BASEBALL
IS IN MY DNA

*A History of Baseball in
Freehold, New Jersey
1857–1973*

GLENN CASHION

RGC PUBLISHING
MIDDLETOWN, NEW JERSEY

Baseball Is in My DNA
A History of Baseball in Freehold, New Jersey 1857–1973

Copyright © 2022 by Glenn Cashion

Published by RGC Publishing
Middletown, New Jersey

For information, contact:
Stellar Communications Houston
www.stellarwriter.com
281-804-7089

Paperback ISBN: 9798987295106
Library of Congress Control Number: 2022921525

Baseball Is in My DNA

"If, like me, you feel a deep connection to the sport of baseball and the town of Freehold, you'll enjoy this well-researched, carefully reported book. Glenn does a fine job compiling the history of the game and telling it through the experience of one family that contributed so much. It's a solid addition to any sports library."

—**MARK HYMAN,** *Director, Shirley Povich Center for Sports Journalism, Merrill College of Journalism, University of Maryland; Co-author of* Confessions of a Baseball Purist

"A history of Freehold baseball with the insight of a historian, the pen of a sportswriter, and the passion of a fan. Glenn, a stand-out player as were his father and brother, has the personal presence and familial insight of over a half century that enables him to present a "you are there" experience, and he does. His extensively researched work gives an insider's account of Freehold fanaticism over baseball that only Glenn can provide. Glenn also offers a candid profile of the Cashion family. Life, not a game of balls and strikes, plays out as a series of triumphs and tragedies as Glenn takes you through the events that formed the family. The reader is not only there on the historic trail of Freehold baseball, but is accompanied each step by the Cashions."

—**RANDALL GABRIELAN,** *Appointed Historian, County of Monmouth*

"Glenn's enthusiasm for baseball comes shining through in this book, and his exuberance is matched in hundreds of Freehold families who have loved the sport for more than one hundred years. With his great love of history, Glenn has done a masterful job of creating a Freehold-focused drama, but we all know this story has played out it many small towns across America as well."

—**LILLIAN G. BURRY,** *Monmouth County Commissioner*

"Glenn's chronicle of Freehold's baseball history is an excellent, well-written story. I am proud of Glenn for bringing to life a part of Freehold's baseball saga that most of us didn't know. He has highlighted a wonderful era that I particularly enjoyed because I played alongside my boyhood idol, Dem Cashion. Kudos to him."

—**HONORABLE RALPH STEINBERG,** *Retired Judge of Tampa, Florida; Former member of the Freehold Merchant baseball team*

"They've been playing baseball in some form in Freehold, New Jersey, for years and years. No one can tell you exactly how many—such was the game's rudimentary beginnings—but Glenn can tell you action was taking place on the diamond in this Monmouth County seat well before America's Civil War. Did baseball in Freehold actually antedate baseball in Cooperstown, New York? Maybe, just maybe, Glenn will tell you. But he's willing to settle for 1857 as a likely beginning. Although no formal records have been found of the game's origins in this Central New Jersey town, Glenn's insightful writings span a 116-year period, 1857-1973. The Cashion family has been actively involved in so much of that baseball in Freehold for so many of those years. So no one is better equipped to tell this story. Glenn writes: 'While cricket still had the most followers, national fervor for baseball was starting to rise.' 'On December 5, 1856, the New York Mercury had referred to the game for the first time as the National Pastime.' And Freehold, New Jersey—like so many other American communities—soon became a hotbed of the action. It's a lively story that tells you the story of the game that still captivates the nation. Glenn tells that story so well; it's a perfect blend of sports, history, and Americana."

—ELLIOTT DENMAN, *Former sports columnist of*
Asbury Park Press *and Olympic racewalker*

This book is lovingly dedicated to those who trod the base paths before me, particularly my family. I thank you for both your skill and your passion, and for your role in creating a keen sense of community in this small, hardworking town.

CONTENTS

PREFACE

"Why don't you write a book?"

If I was asked this question once by my friends, I was asked it a thousand times over the past few decades. Many of my friends have written historical books or personal memoirs. I always replied to this question with "I will sometime in the future."

About twenty years ago, I finally started to diligently research my family history, and I realized that there might be an interesting story to document. As I began to trace my historical roots in Freehold, New Jersey, I quickly realized that there was a common denominator inherent in my family tree. The common denominator present from the late 1880s to the mid-1970s was baseball. I therefore decided to concentrate on the Freehold baseball story, leaving my family history for my next endeavor.

Freehold has demonstrated a commitment to our national pastime for more than one hundred years. It began in the schoolyard of the Freehold Institute and quickly branched out to the formation of numerous teams in the latter half of the nineteenth century and scores of teams in the twentieth century.

Enthusiastic baseball players, led by dedicated and determined managers, exhibited their prowess several times a week during Freehold's peak baseball era. Men, women, and children cheered on their fathers, brothers, and uncles on the baseball fields at Broadway, South Street, Manalapan Avenue, Freehold Driving Park, Lincoln Place, Freehold High School, Intermediate School, and several other ball fields.

There were many average ball players, some eccentric ball players, and some great ball players. The Freehold community loved each and every player. Hundreds of boys and men, and at times a few women, played baseball on Freehold's diamonds during the past century. The Freehold clubs won numerous championships.

This narrative has attempted to capture the vast baseball history of Freehold from 1857 to 1973, when my brother and outstanding pitcher, "Dem," had his last turn at bat. During this period, my family was involved in Freehold baseball for eighty-six consecutive years, starting in 1887. We were players, managers, coaches, and umpires.

The story of Freehold baseball is not unique; other small towns in America went through similar baseball growth spurts. However, I believe Freehold's enthusiasm was unparalleled. Clearly, for my family it was practically a way of life; it was what you did.

I hope I have done justice in my exposition of the history of Freehold baseball. Any errors are entirely attributed to yours truly. I have relied extensively on a plethora of newspaper articles. Several of my teammates offered their reflections on their playing days.

Among those teammates who provided input were Roger Kane, Frank Accisano, Harvey Whille, Barry Drusene, Mike Schottland, Gene Glum, Fred "Booby" Quinn, and Wayne

Cashion. Ralph Steinberg, one of Freehold's pitching stars, graciously offered his memories of his playing days with my brother Dem.

I also offer a special thanks to Carl Beams for lending his photography talents. Additionally, I am very grateful to my friends at the Monmouth County Historical Association.

The sections of the book that discuss the history of Freehold's Black baseball teams and players were brought to life with vivid recollections by Norma Randolph and Roberta Schanck.

I want to thank the many readers who provided sage comments on my early drafts. Special thanks to my wife, Karen, for her patience and support while I labored over this work for the past two years.

My sometimes rambling prose was greatly enhanced by the adroit skill and dedication of Tracey Timpanaro. She was an invaluable asset. Likewise, my sincere thanks to Ella Ritchie and the staff of Stellar Communications Houston, who provided the professional skill and guidance to bring this story to publication.

Glenn Cashion

INTRODUCTION

*"One constant through all the years has been baseball.
America has rolled by like an army of steamrollers.
It's been erased like a blackboard, rebuilt, and
erased again. But baseball has marked the time.
This field, this game—it's a part of our past.
It reminds us of all that once was good,
and it could be again."*
—FIELD OF DREAMS

Throughout many small towns in America in the post–Civil War era, baseball became a prominent community activity, and the baseball fever continued to grow for the next one hundred years. In Freehold, New Jersey, baseball became a social and competitive outlet for many residents.

I grew up in Freehold and remained there until I was twenty-nine (with absences for college and the United States Marine Corps). When I was growing up in the 1940s and 1950s, Freehold was a small rural town with a population of approximately 7,200. I knew that the town's historical roots dated back to the Revolutionary War and the pivotal Battle of Monmouth.

I also knew that there was a baseball game every Sunday afternoon on the Lincoln Place field, one block from my home. I didn't know, but later discovered through extensive research, that Freehold became a baseball stronghold shortly after the game became popular in New Jersey in the mid-1800s. Along with the treasure trove of baseball history, I also learned that my family had been participating in baseball since the late 1800s—managing, umpiring, and even excelling. The story of the evolution of baseball in Freehold is also a chronicle of my family.

I didn't start playing baseball until I was nine years old. My neighborhood friends and I played on the gravel yard behind my grammar school, St. Rose of Lima, which was only about three hundred feet from my house. A bat toss was used to choose sides: a player from one side would toss the bat to a player from the other side, who would clasp the bat with one hand. A player from the other side would place his hand tightly on top of that hand, and they would continue upward alternately until one of the players reached the top of the bat.

If the last player's hand was below the knob of the bat, that player would have to hold the knob and twirl the bat around his head three times. If he retained a hold of the bat, he got to pick the first player, and they alternated picking names thereafter. If he dropped the bat during the twirl, the first pick went to the other player. This "picking sides" process, with slight variations, had started back in the late 1890s. Like many aspects of baseball, traditions go back generations.

I attended many of those Sunday games, along with hundreds of other spectators. I also knew that my brother, David ("Dem"), was a pitcher for the local team. What I did not comprehend at that time was the baseball fervor of the town, nor did I appreciate the community's admiration for my brother.

Late in 1949, Dem began to coach me in the backyard of my home on McLean Street. Within a year, I was the catcher on the St. Rose of Lima team in the newly formed Farm Belt League, the precursor to Freehold's Little League, and I played on various baseball teams for the next eighteen years. My role in Freehold's baseball history is minor compared to the rich history of my ancestors and many other Freehold denizens who played the game for over a century.

Chapter 1

BASEBALL BEGINNINGS

*"God forbid that any balls but those of the Cricket
and Base Ball field may be caught, either
on the fly or on the bound."*
—HENRY CHADWICK, 1861

I n 1966, I spent an incredible three months at the Otesaga Hotel in Cooperstown, New York, participating in an intensive data communications training course. To my delight, I was living in the birthplace of baseball—or so I thought. The birth of baseball has been widely attributed to Abner Doubleday in Cooperstown in 1839.

The story goes that one summer afternoon, local boys were playing a game of town ball, with no clear rules; all hits were fair, and they frequently ran into each other. Doubleday allegedly set down rules for this town ball and invented baseball.[1]

This theory of baseball's American birth was promoted by A. G. Spalding, a pitcher, manager, and influential executive. A contrarian view, promoted by English-born sportswriter Henry Chadwick, known as "the father of baseball," was that this new baseball game was simply a brand of rounders, a British game.

In an attempt to resolve the issue, a select commission was established in 1905, led by Abraham Mills. The Mills Commission interviewed many ball players and so-called eyewitnesses to the events of 1839. The commission's decision, rendered in 1908, stipulated that the Doubleday theory was correct.

Spalding didn't hesitate to publicize this outcome in his 1908 baseball guide. Chadwick, unfortunately, died in April of 1908 and was not able to refute the Mills Commission's faulty conclusion, and it has lingered in baseball lore for decades. Doubleday was, in fact, at West Point in 1839, and he never claimed to have had anything to do with baseball.

Henry Chadwick was known as the Father of Baseball. Frank Pearsall, photographer; A. G. Spalding Collection, New York Library

The myth of Doubleday and Cooperstown, as prescribed by the Mills Commission, came from the memory of Abner Graves, a seventy-three-year-old mining engineer. He submitted a letter to the commission stating that he saw Doubleday "invent" or establish the rules of baseball. Adding to the frail nature of the report was the fact that

Mills knew Doubleday and had never discussed the game's origin with him before Doubleday died in 1893.[2]

The game of baseball, as we know it today, has evolved; it was not invented. There are various points in time when the rules of the game have changed. One can also find evidence of variations of the game. Baseball has rudiments of both cricket, a game divided into innings and supervised by an umpire, and rounders, a children's stick-and-ball game brought to New England by the early colonists. Ball games were called "old cat," "one old cat," "two old cat," "goal ball," "town ball," "stick ball," "round ball," "base," and "base ball."[3]

Children and young men played these baseball variations beginning in the late eighteenth century. "Colonel Jas. Lee, elected member of the Knickerbocker Club in 1846, said that he had often played the game when a boy, and at that time, he was a man of sixty or more years. Dr. Oliver Wendell Holmes, several years since, said to the reporter of a Boston paper that base-ball was one of the sports of his college days at Harvard. Dr. Holmes graduated in 1829."[4]

Princeton University banned ball playing in 1787 as "low and unbecoming gentlemen students . . . an exercise attended with great danger." Henry Wadsworth Longfellow, attending Bowdoin College in 1824, seemed to espouse a different view. He wrote "There is nothing now heard of, in our leisure hours, but ball, ball, ball. I cannot prophesy with any degree of accuracy concerning the continuance of this rage for play, but the effect is good, since there has been a thoroughgoing reformation from inactivity and turpitude."[5]

While "base-ball" variations were peaking with Philadelphia "town ball" and New England "rounders-type ball," there became a nexus of ball playing in New York City in the early 1840s. In the Manhattan area of New York City, a group of gentlemen got together on weekends to engage in one or another version of the game. From 1842 to 1845, these "matches" were held with no rules.

In September 1845, a new participant joined the group. Alexander Joy Cartwright, a twenty-five-year-old shipping clerk, had observed the unruly play for some time. He came prepared with a carefully crafted diagram and plan, based on many ideas of past players. Cartwright's plan stipulated men stationed at first, second, and third base, around a perfect square of ninety feet between bases. A man would be stationed between second and third, called a shortstop. No longer would a base runner be out by being hit by a thrown ball.

Additionally, flat bases would be used. There would be nine players on each side. The batters, or "strikers," would bat in a certain order, which was announced before the game started. The new rule of "three hands out, all out" was introduced, replacing the cricket rule whereby one side continued to bat until the whole team was out. The gentlemen established the New York Knickerbocker Base Ball Club, named after a volunteer fire company to which Cartwright and several other players belonged.[6]

With the assistance of the Knickerbockers' president, Daniel Lucius "Doc" Adams, Cartwright codified the rules and "invented baseball."[7]

The Knickerbocker team began to take the ferry to Hoboken, where more open fields were available for their base-ball matches. They played on an area called the Elysian Fields. On June 19, 1846, the New York Knickerbockers were pitted against the New York Base Ball Club and played, for the first time, under the new rules. The Knickerbockers lost 23–1.

THE FIRST RULES OF BASE BALL,
adopted by the Knickerbocker Club in 1845, are as follows:

SECTION 1. The base shall be from "Home" to second base 42 paces, from first to third base 42 paces equidistant.

SECTION 2. The game to consist of 21 counts or aces, but at the conclusion an equal number of hands must be played.

SECTION 3. The ball must be pitched and not thrown for the bat.

SECTION 4. A ball knocked outside the range of the first or third base is foul.

SECTION 5. Three balls being struck at and missed, and the last one caught, is a hand out; if not caught, is considered fair and the striker bound to run.

SECTION 6. A ball being struck or tipped, and caught either flying or on the first bound, is a hand out.

SECTION 7. A player, running the bases, shall be out, if the ball is in the hands of an adversary on the base, as the runner is touched by it before he makes his base-it being understood, however, that in no instance is a ball to be thrown *at him*.

SECTION 8. A player running, who shall prevent an adversary from catching or getting the ball before making his base, is a hand out.

SECTION 9. If two hands are already out, a player running home at the time a ball is struck, cannot make an ace if the striker is caught out.

SECTION 10. Three hands out, all out.

SECTION 11. Players must take their strike in regular turn.

SECTION 12. No ace or base can be made on a foul strike.

SECTION 13. A runner cannot be put out in making one base, when a baulk is made by the pitcher.

SECTION 14. But one base allowed when the ball bounds out of the field when struck.[8]

By 1857, several clubs were playing by the Knickerbocker rules. However, modifications to the original rules were made. The winning club was changed from the first to get twenty-one aces to the club ahead at the end of nine innings. The ball was made heavier; thus, more balls were hit to the infield, and the shortstop position, created by Doc Adams, was moved into the infield. There would be nine men on a side, and the bases would be set ninety feet apart. In 1883, overhead pitching was permitted.

Before the pitcher's mound was introduced in 1893, there was a five-and-a-half-foot-long box on flat ground. The pitcher could put his back foot anywhere along the four-foot back line of the box, which was 55½ feet from home plate. In 1893, the pitcher's box was replaced with a raised mound and a rubber slab that was twelve inches long (this setup was relocated back to 60½ feet from home plate). From its inception, the height of the pitcher's mound has varied, although a maximum of fifteen inches was stipulated. In 1968, the height of the pitcher's mound was reduced to ten inches.

The fascination with this new American sport, especially in the New York area, reached the general population via the media. While cricket still had the most followers, national fervor for baseball was starting to rise. On December 5, 1856, the *New York Mercury* had referred to the game for the first time as "the National Pastime."[9] The aforementioned Chadwick, a British-born newspaperman who started out as a cricket enthusiast, became a baseball advocate and even played shortstop for the Knickerbockers.

Chadwick was instrumental in having the *New York Times* and other dailies publish baseball results. He also introduced the baseball box score to measure players' results.[10] His early baseball publications had a large following, for example, his 1860 *Base-Ball Player: A Compendium of the Game.*

Another baseball player turned author during this time was John Montgomery Ward. Ward started as a pitcher with Providence, Rhode Island at the age of eighteen in 1878. He went 22–13 in his rookie season, and then in 1879 boosted the Grays to the World Championship with a 47–19 record. On June 17, 1880, Ward pitched the second perfect game, five days after John Lee Richmond pitched the first. He was a

JOHN M. WARD.
ALLEN & GINTER'S
RICHMOND. Cigarettes VIRGINIA.

John Montgomery Ward; Allen & Ginter's Cigarettes baseball card, United States Library of Congress

Columbia-trained lawyer and used his literary talents to write several important documents.

His *Base-Ball: How to Become a Player*, written in 1888, is one of the best books about baseball ever written by a player. "The book is a wonderful window on an era that we all too often regard as quaint—when we don't ignore it altogether. In many ways, the game isn't that different than almost one-hundred-fifty years ago. In his book, Ward describes the brushback (with pitchers throwing from 55½ feet). He discusses the hit-and-run (without naming it), playing the infield in, pitching signs, and the pick-off. He affirms that bases are stolen by the pitcher, not the catcher, and he treats the question of whether a curve ball curves as a settled matter."[11] Ward's instructional chapters are each devoted to a particular baseball position, and he also covers the batter, the base runner, and curve pitching.

With a more formalized, rules-oriented game and the public becoming increasingly interested in the game, baseball teams began to sprout up, particularly in urban areas and educational institutions. Soldiers played baseball during the Civil War, and they continued to participate in ball clubs upon their return from the military. During the Gilded Age, baseball's growth was phenomenal.

The Elysian Fields was only one of many baseball fields in New Jersey in the mid to late 1850s. Urban areas with good railroad access were prime locations for teams to play their ball games. However, smaller, less urban towns with excellent railroad access also began to lure spectators to baseball games. In the 1860 census, Newark was the eleventh-largest city in the United States. By this time, New Jersey had 177 ball clubs in twenty-one municipalities, and Newark had fifty-two clubs.[12] Intercollegiate baseball began on July 1, 1859, when Amherst defeated Williams 73–32, played under the rules of the Massachusetts game (the name by which town ball was known in New England). Princeton began its baseball life in 1864 and in 1866 beat Rutgers 40–2.

With the Garden State's baseball enthusiasm in the 1850s, it wasn't long before the small town of Freehold, New Jersey, would catch baseball fever.

Chapter 2

1857-1900: FREEHOLD EMBRACES BASEBALL

*"I see great things in baseball.
It's our game—the American game."*
—WALT WHITMAN

In the 1800s, baseball had a relatively smooth start in Freehold, although an errant pitch did break a nose in at least one game, and in another instance, the father of the umpire had to pull his gun to stop an angry mob from accosting his child.

It should also be noted that the Freehold newspapers were aware that baseball was being played in nearby locales and didn't hesitate to issue some words of encouragement to residents in 1857:

"One of the things most wanted in this village is some provision for gymnastic exercises. There are a large number of youth and young men, whose occupations and habits are sedentary, who would be healthier and happier for judicious, wholesome outdoor exercise and amusement. One of the prettiest, cheapest, most healthful, and most universally popular games we know of is ball playing. A well-organized base-ball or cricket club would be a capital thing, and likely save several doctor's bills besides. Similar clubs live and flourish in other villages; have we not spirit enough to get up one here? What say the clerks and the boys? Where are the Freehold athletes?"[1]

The Freehold Base Ball Club was formed within a year with twenty members. An interesting tidbit about the first secretary of the club, A. S. Lokerson, is that he was the proprietor of Freehold's Segar Shop, which offered superior "segars," tobacco, snuff, and pipes. While there exists no record of the team's performance, the team started with a solid moral code: "Any member using vulgar or profane language upon the ground shall be fined a sum not over one dollar and suspended from playing until the same be paid."[2] The team met twice a week behind Hudson Bennett's house.

During the Civil War years, there was no record of baseball being played in Freehold. However, the game did not lose any impetus. "Considering the widespread popularity of various forms of premodern baseball and the emergence of the 'New York game' during the 1850s, it is not surprising that many soldiers carried bats and balls in their knapsacks during the Civil War . . . Ball matches helped recruits pass the days and months between battles, and these spirited contests amused inmates in Union and Confederate prisons."[3]

The local media in 1865 again called for more ball players: "Base-ball is the mania now with our juveniles. Two clubs are organized in Freehold, and every Saturday afternoon they indulge in a game of friendly rivalry on Professor Woodhull's school grounds. It would be a good idea if the 'children of larger growth' would adopt this athletic sport occasionally . . . We should like to see some movement in the matter among our young men."[4] William W. Woodhull, principal, and Charles F. Woodhull, vice principal, led Monmouth School, which was a boarding school whose mission was to prepare boys for college or business.[5]

Fearful Knocks

One of the earliest baseball "matches" box scores was recorded on November 24, 1865. The Freehold Institute fielded the early baseball teams. Over the next several years, the Institute had various team designations and sometimes fielded their "first nines" and other times fielded their "second nines." On this particular day, the Institutes played the Atlantics at the Fair Grounds, with Institute the victor 25–23. A local newspaper reporter highlighted the game with this report: "Pitching on both sides was very good and W. E. Denise's knocks were 'fearful' on the one side, while Messers McGrath and Sours play was fully equal to first-rate playing."[6]

A return match of the above teams on March 23, 1866, this time of both "second nines," resulted in a 30–17 victory for the Atlantics. In this box score, one notes the standard identification of the names of the umpire and the scorer. Also, the box score notes the name and number of "fly catchers" on each side, which was a standard notation in the early days of newspaper reporting.[7]

The Freehold Institute celebrated its fifty years of operation in 1894. It was one of the best-known preparatory schools in the state. Approximately one hundred alumni celebrated in Randolph Hall at the school on this anniversary date and continued their celebratory festivities at the American Hotel. Among the graduates in attendance were several New Jersey judges, the Honorable David Demarest Denise (1859), Henry Allaire (1862), Joseph A. Yard of the Monmouth Democrat (1887), DuBois Marris, and R. V. Lawrence of Freehold.[8]

ON AUGUST 8, 1867, "B. P." WROTE AN ARTICLE IN THE LOCAL FREEHOLD NEWSPAPER:

SOMETHING FOR THE ADMIRER OF BASE BALL, AS A BASE BALLIST.

IT CAME ABOUT THUS. Secondary deployment is too shirksome for the system. The doctor said we needed exercise. Doctor knows. He told us to Join Base Ball. We joined. Bought a book of instructions and for five days we studied it wisely and well. Then we bought a sugar-scoop cap, a red belt, a green shirt, yellow trousers, pumpkin-colored shoes, a paper collar and purple neck tie, and, with a lot of other delegates, moved gently to the ground.

There were two nines. These nines are antagonists. The ball is a pretty little drop of softness, the size of a goose egg, and five degrees harder than a brick. The two nines play against each other. It is a quiet game, much like chess, only a little more chase than chess.

There was an umpire. His position was a hard one. He sits on a box and yells 'foul.' His duty is severe.

The umpire said 'play.' It is the most radical play I know of, this base ball. Sawing cord wood is moonlight rambles beside base ball. So the pitcher sent a ball toward me. It looked pretty coming, so I let it come. Then he sent another. I hit with the club, and dove it gently upward. The ball lit in the pitcher, or his hands, and somebody said he caught a fly. Alas, poor fly! I walked leisurely toward the base. Another man took the bat. I turned to see how he was making it, and a mule kicked me on the cheek. The man said it was the ball. It felt like a mule, and I reposed on the grass. The ball went on!

My next time to strike, the umpire yelled, 'Brick to bat.' The pitcher sent in one hip high. I missed it. He sent another neck high. It struck me in the gullet. 'Foul' yelled the umpire. He sent in the ball again. This time I took it square and sent it down the right field, through a parlor window—a kerosene lamp …. Then I slung the bat and meandered forth to the first base. I heard high words and looked. When I slung the bat I had with it broken the jaw of the umpire and was fined ten cents.

That was an eventful chap who first invented base ball. It's such fun. I have played five games, and this is the glowing result:

Twenty-seven dollars paid out for things.

One bunged eye, badly bunged.

One broken little finger.

One bump on the head.

Nineteen lame backs.

A sore jaw.

One thumb dislocated.

Three sprained ankles.

Five swelled legs.

One dislocated shoulder, from trying to throw a ball a thousand yards.

Two hands raw from trying to stop hot balls.

I have played two weeks, and don't think I like the game. There is not a square inch on, in or under me but aches. I sleep nights dreaming of hot balls, 'flys,' 'fouls,' and descending 'sky rockets.' I never worked so hard since Ruth stole wheat and never was so lame since the burning of Luther . . . But I am proud of my proficiency in the game.

Bawlingly thine, 'Brick' Pomeroy

P.S. All ladies in favor of 'universal suffering' are invited to join our club.[9]

The Freehold Institute baseball team most often is identified as either the "Institute" or, in the early 1870s, as the Nantihala Base Ball Club. The latter team name is one of many unique names in Freehold's nineteenth-century baseball history. Nantahala is a Cherokee name, not of New Jersey Indian heritage. There is a Nantahala National Forest and a Nantahala River in North Carolina. The name means "Land of the Noonday Sun." Why a Freehold team would adopt a version of this name remains a mystery.

The Monmouth Base Ball team began playing circa 1867 and continued operating via a few reorganizations until the early 1890s. The earliest recorded box score was in August 1867. On August 16, at the Metropolitan Grounds in Long Branch, the Monmouth Club was victorious over the Sea

Side Club of Long Branch 27–9. The Long Branch Club hosted the Monmouth Club with a dinner at Hendrickson's Hotel.

Bountiful Batting

On August 19, the return match between these two clubs was held at the Freehold Fair Grounds. The Monmouth Club soundly defeated Sea Side 69–27. "Some splendid specimens of batting were exhibited on both sides. As was the custom, the clubs sat down to a sumptuous dinner prepared for their discussion by the worthy best of the American Hotel, and soon the contest of bat and ball was exchanged for an investigation of the merits of the many good things which were spread before them. That the dinner was a success was plainly shown by the tribute which the exponents of muscular activity paid to their appetites."[10]

One of the earliest baseball reorganizations in Freehold baseball history—and there were many subsequent ones—occurred on May 1, 1872. The Monmouth Base Ball Club reorganization was held in the office of J. L. Howell, who was named chairman.

"The club has some excellent players and may expect to compete successfully with the first amateur clubs of the State ... Nearly seventy-five honorary members are about to join the club."[11]

The 1872 Monmouth Base Ball Club pennant is shown flying with Old Glory. Courtesy of Cashion archives

With the Monmouth Base Ball Club reorganized, Freehold boasted six baseball clubs: Andes, Atlantics, Dolly Vardens, Independents, Nantihalas, and Monmouth. In June, the Monmouth Club met the Nantihalas at the Monmouth grounds and soundly defeated them 40–8. The field was in excellent shape and, according to local reports, the match was loudly cheered by the many spectators. There was "scarcely a muff or failure by the Monmouth batsmen." A large flagpole, generously furnished by J. F. T. Foreman Jr., had been raised. On the pole flew the national colors, surmounted by the pennant of the club, a white streamer bound with blue, bearing a large *M*.

During that same week, the Nantihala team left Freehold at eight a.m. for Hightstown and engaged the Hightstown Resolute team, defeating them 42–22. The team returned home that evening, and, to the delight of the players, Rev. Chambers, principal of the Institute, took them out for ice cream.[12]

Matches between Freehold teams and nearby towns, including New Jersey colleges, were common during this era. Also, it was not unusual for teams to use local substitutes in order to achieve a full nine-player roster.

On June 12, 1872, many spectators assembled at the Monmouth Grounds to witness the match between the university nine of Princeton College and the Monmouths. The Princeton team played with only eight players, and the Monmouths had to have local substitutes to complete their team. The Princeton team defeated the Monmouths 23–18. "The playing on both sides was very fair, but few muffs or overthrows being made. The strangers were hospitably entertained by the Monmouths at their respective homes."[13]

The following week the Atlantic ball club played a match game of eight innings, lasting five hours, against

The 1876 Nantihala baseball team was one of the earliest Freehold teams. Courtesy of Ken Rosen collection

the Centrals, of the Colts Neck Base Ball Club, at the Colts Neck grounds. While the Centrals were much older than the Atlantics, the Atlantics were the victors 55–24.

A Solid Blanking

Later that year, in October, the Rutgers College nine had a match game with the Nantihalas on the Nantihalas' grounds. The Rutgers nine went home with the victory 21–12. The New Brunswick Times reported: "The 'glorious uncertainties' of base ball are proverbial. For some time past, the Rutgers College nine have experienced only its inglorious certainties. Saturday was the day appointed for their game with the Nantihala Club of Freehold but, when the time for departure came, only four of the nine put in an appearance. Some were necessarily absent; the courage of others had oozed out—like Bob Acres—at their fingers' ends, and they had absconded to parts unknown . . . On arrival at Freehold, the prospects grew steadily darker. The Nantihala Club, in some way that was dark, had re-inforced their nine by adding three men outside of the school, Hageman, pitcher of the Princetons, Howell, short stop of the Trentons, and Cooper, first baseman of the Monmouths. The Rutgers nine went into the game on the 'hurrah' principle, and by sheer force of impudence, blanked their opponents."[14]

A short-lived baseball team was the Dolly Vardens. Two box scores are shown for match games with the Central team of the Colts Neck Base Ball Club, in September and October of 1872. The Dolly Vardens were victorious in both games. They used the grounds of the Monmouth Base Ball Club and even used umpires from Monmouth.[15]

Dolly Varden was a character in *Barnaby Rudge*, one of two historical novels penned by Charles Dickens (the other being *A Tale of Two Cities*.) The name Dolly Varden has always been a symbol of feisty endurance.

Dolly Varden was a cultural phenomenon that inspired fashion, theater, song, art, and commerce based on the eponymous coquette concocted by Dickens. Dolly Varden is the second Freehold baseball team name with strange roots.

The Nantihala Club won the Monmouth County Championship in 1873, 1874, and 1876. In 1873, they defeated the Modocs 43–33. In 1874, they defeated the Modocs in a forfeited game 9–0. In 1876, the Nantihala Club defeated the Original Base Ball Club of Keyport 25–14. In this latter game, "the best catch of the day was made by Fred Guerin, of the Nantihalas, who caught a 'liner' with his left hand."[16]

Modoc is another unique team name in Freehold's baseball history. Once again, "Modoc" does not seem to have any relevance to Freehold. The Modoc Indian tribe in 1872 was located in Northern California. Some disputes ensued and war broke out between the Modoc tribe and the United States government. It was the only major Indian war fought in California and the only one in which an Army general was killed. The war lasted from November 29, 1872, until June 1, 1873, and resulted in the fatalities of several Modoc warriors and United States soldiers.[17] The Modoc team was established shortly after the Modoc War, perhaps in sympathy with the Modoc tribe.

The Modoc team operated from 1873 to 1875. They generally fielded a very good team, playing against both Freehold teams and teams from nearby towns.[18]

The Nantihalas continued to dominate up to the early 1880s. The team reorganized in 1874 and handed down a challenge to any baseball club in Monmouth County for the championship of said county. The team looked very neat and workmanlike in their white flannel suits trimmed with red.[19] Another reorganization took place in 1880 and, again, the team challenged any team in Monmouth County. Nothing shy about that team.

However, in 1885 and 1886, the team reverted to being called the Institute and in June 1885 was defeated by Peddie Institute 27–22. Later that month, they redeemed themselves by trouncing the Freehold Town Nine 33–6. During this period, the Freehold Institute promoted its institution with ads identifying the faculty as graduates of Miami University, Lewisburg University, Princeton College, Yale College, and the University of Bonn-on-the-Rhine. Referenced as amusements at the Institute were gymnasium, bowling alley, and Base Ball.[20]

First Old-Timers Game

The Freehold Institute and the Old Monmouth team played an exciting game of ball on June 5, 1886. The original Monmouth team played between 1872 and 1876 and then disbanded. This game was the first "old-timers game" in Freehold's history.

"Much interest was excited in the match and many fair ones assembled to see their fathers, husbands and lovers participate in the game. The Institute nine was composed of the boys who have played so well this year as to secure the championship of the County. . . . Freeman caught three elegant foul flys behind the bat, which made his heart swell with pride. Conover appeared in his nobby knickerbockers and was prepared to mash the field; he did some elegant pitching and was much admired for his superb form. Bennett distinguished himself by endeavoring to make a home run on called balls, but died a natural death at third base. Davis swayed a fly, but excitement caused him to pull the filling out of his cigar, which made him ill; he retired in a blanket. It was notable that whenever a Monmouth man made a run, he did not stop at home plate but invariably ran right into the reserved seat quarter, where he was received so warmly that the Institute boys turned green. The Institute boys won easily 47–12."[21]

The Institute's last recorded game was in 1892.

A team of short operating duration was the Orientals. There are a couple of recorded games for this team in 1877, when they are shown to be a team from the Institute, and in 1887, when their team included substitutes on the starting team. This latter game marks the first appearance of my ancestors in a Freehold baseball game. James "Jim" Fitzgibbon (1866–1958) was the catcher.[22]

Fitzgibbon would later play for the Monmouth Base Ball Club through 1891; he was the son of my grandmother, Ann Garrity, and her first husband, John Fitzgibbon. Jim married Nora Conover of Freehold on March 22, 1891, and then lived in Shrewsbury, Red Bank, and Point Pleasant. Jim continued to be involved with baseball and in 1903 became manager of the Red Bank nine.

The year 1887 also marked the somewhat brief attempt by the Monmouth Club to resume its playing days. They fielded a decent team and were part of the Monmouth Base Ball League. At the Monmouth County Amateur Club organization meeting in Red Bank, Messrs. Conover and Rue were the Monmouth team representatives. Reminiscent of the "Old Monmouth" Club of 1872, "two handsome foul flags adorned the baseball field of the Monmouth Athletic Association. They were made of white flannel, faced with cardinal red, the colors of the club. Upon the white ground of the flags, were the letters 'M.A.A.' in cardinal red . . . the work on them was done by several of their young lady friends who are admirers of the national game and take an interest in the matches played by the Freehold boys."[23]

On June 21, 1887, the Monmouth team beat the Keyport nine 22–9. "Seven innings were played, the visitors having to take the 5:30 train home." On August 12, 1887, the Monmouth team came up short against the City of Long

Branch 21–13. The Monmouths also lost to the Highlands Indians on August 9, 1887, by the score of 12–9. The team's loss was partially explained by the uneven ground; the Indians batted all 'grounders' which bounced in such a way that the fielders could not pick them up. Fitzgibbon was credited with a two-base hit in this match.[24]

Pulling a Gun

At the end of the 1887 baseball season, a fascinating game was held on the grounds in Red Bank. Monmouth was pitted against the Eurekas. According to the local newspaper, "The crowd assembled seemed to applaud whenever they made a good play and to hiss the umpire, Mr. Tom Arrowsmith, a Freehold resident, and the Monmouths when a point was scored against them. This went on until it became disgraceful. When the Monmouths ran up the score in the third inning to 9, one man out in the crowd began throwing apples and sticks at the umpire, and another cried, 'Mob him!' and the crowd rushed towards him. Mr. Arrowsmith's father was standing near him, and when the mob started for his son, he drew a revolver and said: 'The first one who touches him gets shot!' At this the crowd began to scatter and no blows were struck. The umpire had called play several times and when the Eurekas, who were in the field, refused to play for over 5 minutes, he announced the game won by the Monmouths, by a score of 9–0. The Red Bank crowd evidently thought that they would scare the Freehold boys and run them off the field, but they did not scare worth a cent and were the last to leave."[25]

The year 1888 brought an unusual hiatus of baseball activity in Freehold. The Monmouth team did not organize due to player injuries and general lack of interest. They would be reborn during a banner baseball year in 1891. In July, at the Fair Grounds, there was a game between the nine from Manasquan and the Freehold Cyclers. While this was the first, and perhaps the only, game played by the Freehold Cyclers, they managed to play well and won the game 36–10.[26]

By 1891, baseball was the talk of the town. New teams were organized and reorganized. Managers were named and then resigned, with new managers named. Local businesses started to have their own teams. Women were reported to attend games and "add greatly to the tone of the assembled." There was even a willingness to pay to attend games—ten cents per person at one July game.

The Freehold Athletic Association Base-ball Club was formed in May 1891, but within a month the name was changed to the Monmouth Baseball Club, recognizing the Monmouth team of 1887.[27]

Manager Harry Thompson didn't last long in his role, perhaps because his occupation as a salesman for Singer Sewing Machines was so successful. In July, he resigned and Thomas V. Arrowsmith (of previously mentioned umpiring fame) was elected to fill the vacancy.[28] The newly constituted Monmouth Baseball Club would continue operating until mid-1893.

Freehold's surging baseball enthusiasm continued when Michael Welsh, Charles Humann, and Webb Williams met to organize another team (with "baseball" now becoming common vernacular for the game) in May 1891. Three different team names were given by the three organizers, all claiming it was the right one. The three options were the Keg Drainers, the Freehold Temperance Baseball Club (exciting choices), and the Wild Ducks. The latter name was the accepted choice—another unique name in Freehold baseball legend. Charles Humann, a butcher on South Street, was named manager, and the Wild Ducks had a successful playing life span of three years.[29]

The Wild Ducks made it known that they would not play baseball on Sunday. Michael Welsh was an active member of the Catholic Benevolent League and may have had some influence on this issue. Thus, they played their ball games on Saturdays. They defeated the Englishtown nine 15–5 in May 1892, and they lost to the Monmouths the following Saturday 20–17. It was in this game that Thompson, who was playing second base, and the Wild Ducks' pitcher, Valadier, got into a heated argument, and the two hot-headed gentlemen were parted before they had punished each other very severely.[30]

Appearing in their brand-new uniforms on Saturday, July 4, 1891, the Wild Ducks "crossed bats" with the Colts Neck nine and came out the winner 17–8. The new suits were grey, with cardinal red stockings and belts and a red duck on the shirtfront.[31]

That Had to Hurt

On that same day, Freehold held two other baseball contests. The Monmouths entertained the Brooklyn Mechanics on the South Street grounds. The attendance was large, and an admission fee of ten cents was charged.

John DeRoche was hit in the face by a pitched ball and suffered a broken nose. Also, the Monmouths' pitcher incurred a minor hand injury and had to be replaced by a spectator. "Mr. James A. Joeck, of Newark, came out in the field and turned up his trousers over patent leather shoes, rolled up the sleeves of a freshly laundered bosom shirt, and began very deliberately to throw wildly, letting the first man to base on balls. He was a perfect stranger to all but one or two. At the exhibition of bad pitching, the small boys began to exclaim, 'Look at the dude. He can't pitch.'"[32]

Baseball had begun early that July 4th morning and marked the first time local Freehold businesses would field a team. The game was played on the Broadway grounds and matched the nine from the V. H. Rothschild shirt factory against the Stokes Brothers file factory. The game was won by the file factory 18–12.[33]

Ultimately, Joeck ended up earning his keep. He was elected as a member of the Monmouths and appeared as the pitcher in a contest on July 15 against the Hightstown Orientals. Fitzgibbon continued to be the catcher for the Monmouths. They were defeated 15–5.

Joeck and Fitzgibbon served as the battery in another game against the Keyport Stars on August 1, 1891. This game had an attendance estimated to be the largest of any previous game in Freehold. The large attendance of women was also noted. It was held on the Broadway grounds, as the Barkalow grounds on South Street had been given up. Especially note-worthy was the playing of Jamison at shortstop. ". . . for in every game he manages to make a grandstand play or two. They call him 'The Dummy' because he cannot speak or hear. But, as Jimmy White said on Saturday, 'He's medicine! That's a great pair of lights he's got in his head.' There is never a play made that he doesn't see. An instance of his quick perception was a play in the game. He caught a hot liner and threw to second with about the same speed it came to him, making a double play. It was done so quick that everybody gaped for a moment. Then they howled and he grinned."[34]

The ever-changing management of the Monmouths con-tinued on July 24. Arrowsmith resigned because he didn't have enough time to devote to it. Phillip DeRoche, the town hatter, was elected manager.[35]

A battle between the "Old Monmouth" team of 1887 and the "New Monmouth" team of 1891 took place on August 6. The spectators rooted for the "old men," but the revitalized Monmouth team prevailed 19–7.

I'll Be Right Back

The Wild Ducks and the Monmouths played good ball during August and September of '91. The ball players continued to reveal some interesting quirks. On August 10, the Monmouths lost to Toms River by a close score of 14–13. The Monmouth lineup remained pretty much the same, except for one substitution. "Wes Crawford took the place of Harry Thompson in left field for two innings while Harry went up town and sold a sewing machine."[36] Thompson's priorities always seemed to be on sewing machines.

During an abbreviated game with Monmouth against Red Bank at Freehold, the news reported that "one of the visitors 'did a baby,' and ran for his coat several times declaring he wouldn't play because he thought the umpire favored the Freehold nine." The seven-inning game ended with Monmouth on top 10–4.[37]

The worst defeat for the Monmouths came at the hands of the Tabernacles of Jersey City on August 20. Monmouth's pitcher, Joeck, was struck twice in the arm before the game and was unable to pitch. Valadier was brought in to pitch and didn't fare too well. The Tabernacles, a good ball club, easily beat the Monmouths 19–1.

The game between the Wild Ducks and the Monmouths on August 28, 1891, marked a milestone in my ancestral baseball history. Richard McNicholas and his wife and three boys moved from Baltimore to Freehold in the late 1880s. One of the sons, John, was my grandfather. He married Jennie Farrell, my grandmother, on March 17, 1897.

John's brother Michael played a little baseball before getting married and moving to Pennsylvania. John's other brother, Thomas, called "Tony," was a pitching and batting star from 1891 to 1903. The August 28 game had Fitzgibbon on the Monmouth team, while both Michael and Tony McNicholas played on the Wild Ducks team. It was reported as "the prettiest game of baseball which has been played in Freehold this season. The Ducks were victorious 9–6. Young McNicholas pitched the nine innings and struck out seven men."[38]

Doubleheader games became popular at this time. Also, it was becoming more common for New York / Brooklyn teams to journey to Freehold. These games were well attended. On the morning of September 7, 1891, the Brooklyn Barretts were matched against the Monmouths. The starting pitcher was Joeck, with Tony playing center field and relieving Joeck later in the game.

Tony slammed a double during the game. Michael played center field. The familiar names of Crawford, Thompson, Hall, Donaldson, Slattery, Baum, Conover, Welsh, and Freeman made up the remainder of the Monmouth team. Monmouth was victorious 18–3.

In the afternoon game, the Wild Ducks lost to the Brooklyn Ferns 9–7. Most of the same Monmouth players played on the Wild Ducks team, led by Humann, their manager. In this game, Tony pitched the entire game and struck out twelve, while again banging a double.

Another team that formed at the end of 1891 was the Freehold Stars, with Fred Baum as manager and Joseph Laird Jr. as captain.

The Wild Ducks ended their operation at the beginning of the 1892 season. They reorganized (a common phenomenon in Freehold baseball) in March. The new team was the Freehold Baseball Club.[39]

On July 4, 1892, the Monmouth team, now playing on the Fair Grounds, defeated the Unions of New York in a hotly contested game with a score of 4–2. On the same day, on the Broadway grounds, the Freehold club met the Mineola club of Brooklyn and were defeated 5–3.[40]

The DeRoche family continued to oversee the Monmouth Club. At the beginning of the 1893 season, J. F. DeRoche was elected manager and John A. DeRoche assistant manager.[41]

The Shirt Factory nine ventured to Red Bank on May 31, 1893, and won a nicely played ball game 13–8. They lost two games to the Monmouths in June of that year. Perhaps their best game was on June 11, 1897, when they defeated the Oreos of Asbury Park 5–4. The Shirt Factory team battery was Tony McNicholas and Crawford.[42]

Three Notable Games

During the last half of 1893, the Monmouths had a robust schedule. Aside from losing to the Brooklyn Jeromes 13–6 in a poorly played game, and to the New Brunswick nine, they had a long winning streak against Mineola of Brooklyn, Union of New York, Police Gazette of New York, Spring Lake, Montgomery of Jersey City, the Wild Ducks, and the Shirt Factory. They beat Asbury Park for the Monmouth County Championship. Tony McNicholas was the dominant pitcher throughout this period, averaging ten strikeouts per game. Three games during this period are of interest.

The first is the June 24, 1893, game against the Princeton Giants. The Giants, "a nine of colored waiters from the hotels

HALL,   Base Ball—Fair Grounds.   PHOTO.
"VETERANS" vs. "SONS OF REST."
THURSDAY, JULY 15, 1897.

The Veterans took on the Sons of Rest at the fairgrounds on July 15, 1897. From left to right on the front row: unknown player, George Hoffman, Almstead Abrahams, John R. Parker, Fred Bennett, Clifford Snyder. Second row: Tunis Yetman, Andrew Chambers, William Burtis, George Ward, John DeRoche or Ed Bacon (records unclear), Fred Parker, George Freeman, Tom Richardson, E. I. Vanderveer, Florence Conover. Third row: Henry Davis, James Freeman, (unknown first name) Smith, Frank Bridgman, Dr. Harry W. Ingling, John Bawden. Courtesy of Monmouth County Historical Association

of Princeton, had defeated the Monmouths two weeks previously ... The teams were both stronger than before, and the game was one of the best ever played in Freehold, it being anybody's game until the ninth inning. McNicholas pitched a strong game, striking out fifteen men. He struck out five men in succession in the sixth, seventh and eighth innings.

"McNicholas contributed with his bat, getting a double and driving in a run in the eighth inning. In the end, the Princeton Giants prevailed 9–6." Newspaper reporting of baseball at this time and into the future decades was detailed and provided the reader with a good feel for the action. This was the first recorded game of a Black baseball team playing in Freehold.[43]

The second noteworthy game occurred on July 22, 1893, when the Mineola nine of Brooklyn came to the Monmouths in Freehold. "Another victory graces the list of victories won this season by the Monmouth base ball club and another scalp hangs on their belt. It is the scalp of the Mineola nine, who came here last Saturday from the far city of Brooklyn to trail the home team in the dust. But instead, they were not contented with merely defeating them but did not allow them a single run. Those players who were particularly to blame for this state of affairs were Tony McNicholas and Joe Koskey. But two hits were made from the former's delivery while twelve times did Mineola sluggers vainly fan the air. Three times without effort only to find out that Koskey had the ball and that they must make way for another victim."[44] The Monmouths defeated the Mineola nine 8–0. In this era, a shutout was a rare event.

Of interest to Freehold residents is that while Tony McNicholas was mowing down the Mineola batters, another Freehold notable was continuing his success in the cycling world. On that same day in Asbury Park, world cycling champion Arthur Zimmerman competed in a cycling event. He won the quarter-mile and was awarded a $75 diamond. He also won the one-mile race and won a $150 diamond ring.[45]

The third noteworthy Monmouth game during that period was on June 10, 1893, when Monmouth defeated the

William Wesley Crawford is in the top row, third from right on the 1891 Monmouth Baseball Team. Courtesy of Alison Bailey collection

Shirt Factory 23–12. Tony was slightly below par with his pitching, garnering only six strikeouts. However, he made up for it with his slugging. He pounded the ball that day for a double, a triple, and a home run.[46]

Another Freehold team that played between 1892 and 1900 was the Freehold Tigers. This team included William Wesley Crawford, a Prudential insurance agent, who enjoyed playing ball with this young team. On April 21, 1900, the Tigers beat the Farmingdale Mohawks in a slugfest 22–13.[47]

The decade ended with many local Freehold men entering the military during the Spanish-American war. Under Captain Peter Vredenburgh, Tony McNicholas was a private in Company I, 3rd Regiment, New Jersey National Guard.

In July and August of 1898, Company I played ball against the Pompton Plains nine. In July, they lost 8–3, with Tony striking out sixteen batters. In August, they lost 11–7, with Tony striking out nine.[48]

As the nineteenth century closed, the hamlet of Freehold, with a population of 2,900, was ablaze with baseball. The game was no longer only a man's sport. Women were avid spectators and provided refreshments at the games. Men became fans and were never shy about shouting encouragement or a few choice words. A few teams would dominate over the coming decades, and Black ballplayers would become much more common on the Freehold baseball fields, as both visiting teams and local teams. Although my great-uncle Tony would only stay active for a few more years, the Cashion clan would soon become prominent and remain so for the next seven decades as Freehold's baseball environment began to mature.

Chapter 3

1900-1916 BASEBALL TAKES OFF IN FREEHOLD

*"Never let the fear of striking out keep
you from playing the game."*
—BABE RUTH

Matching the changing times, there were some significant changes in the game of baseball in the early part of the twentieth century. Women became avid spectators and sideline workers, Black teams appeared on the local diamonds, attendance began to grow, and devout Christians rallied against the game being played on the holy day. From a Cashion family standpoint, our highlight had to be my dad, David "Dem" Cashion, calling Babe Ruth out on strikes.

The century certainly began on a humorous note. What better way to start off than to have a couple of ball games that pitted the thick and thin men of Freehold against each other. On July 14, 1900, the "Fats" beat the "Thins" by the score of 22–17. The fat men could not run, so running substitutes were used.

On July 28, 1900, another game was held on the Broadway grounds before a good-sized audience. The Thins won the

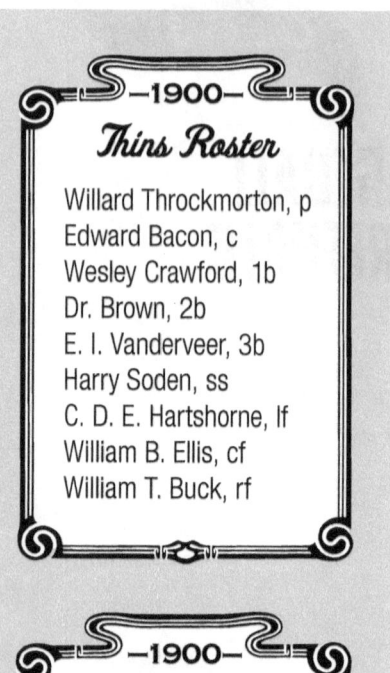

—1900—

Thins Roster

Willard Throckmorton, p
Edward Bacon, c
Wesley Crawford, 1b
Dr. Brown, 2b
E. I. Vanderveer, 3b
Harry Soden, ss
C. D. E. Hartshorne, lf
William B. Ellis, cf
William T. Buck, rf

—1900—

Fats Roster

P. Vredenburgh, p
William F. Barkalow, c
O. B. F. Randolph, 1b
F. A. Brower, 2b
C. C. Snyder, 3b
R. Sterry, ss
T. Richardson, lf
Daniel Smith, cf
Joseph Atkinson, rf
Substitutes:
Thomas Richardson
and Edward Cashion[1]

game by a score of 29–8. At this game, some of the lady friends of the players organized themselves into a Red Cross corps and set up a hospital tent on the grounds—just in case. They also sold ice cream, lemonade, and Sterry's cocoa, which, with the gate receipts, netted over $15.

Baseball team reorganizations also continued to take place. My uncle, Edward Casper Cashion, held a V. H. Rothschild Factory team meeting at his home in May 1901. Several family members were in fact employed at the shirt factory, but Edward worked in the county clerk's office.

Thomas Layton was named secretary and treasurer at this meeting, and Edward was named the manager. His playing days were limited; he primarily served in managerial roles for the next several years.

Another team was formed in June 1901, simply called the "Freehold" team, with William Freeman as manager. The first recorded game of this new team was against a "scrub" team from the Shirt Factory, with the Freehold team winning by a score of 23-11. Errors and bad playing marked the game.

The Freehold team had a challenging game with Matawan on June 8, 1901. Reminiscent of a game played in 1891 with "the dummy" playing second base, this Freehold team had a pitcher named Jones, who was impervious to spectator yawping.

"A snappy game was played on both sides, but the Freeholders seemed to be weak in their stick work. The Freehold rooters were there in great numbers. Those who rooted for Matawan were disappointed very much to find that after yelling for eight innings at the Freehold pitcher, he was deaf and dumb, and had expressions of approval, which spurred him on to more brilliant work with each successive throw."[4] The game ended in a 5-5 tie.

Tony McNicholas's health started to deteriorate in 1901,

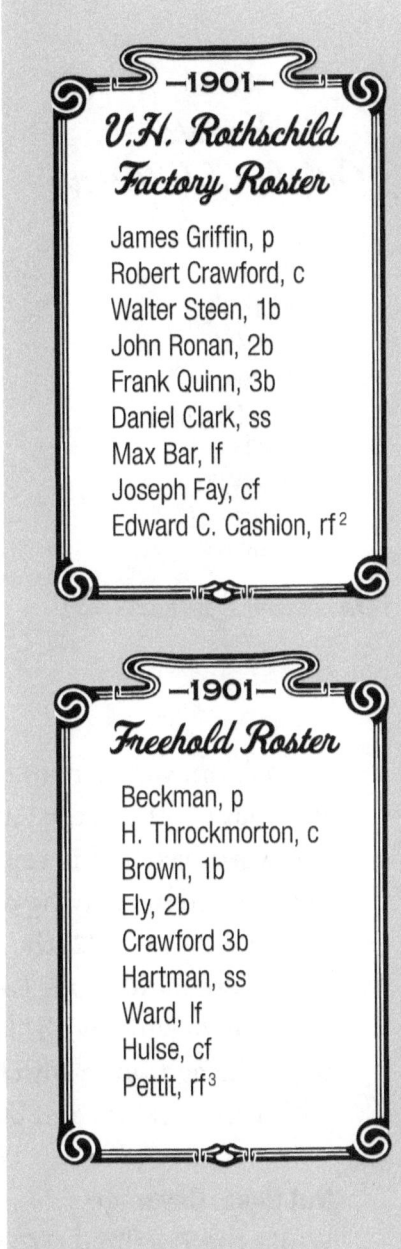

—1901—
V.H. Rothschild Factory Roster

James Griffin, p
Robert Crawford, c
Walter Steen, 1b
John Ronan, 2b
Frank Quinn, 3b
Daniel Clark, ss
Max Bar, lf
Joseph Fay, cf
Edward C. Cashion, rf [2]

—1901—
Freehold Roster

Beckman, p
H. Throckmorton, c
Brown, 1b
Ely, 2b
Crawford 3b
Hartman, ss
Ward, lf
Hulse, cf
Pettit, rf [3]

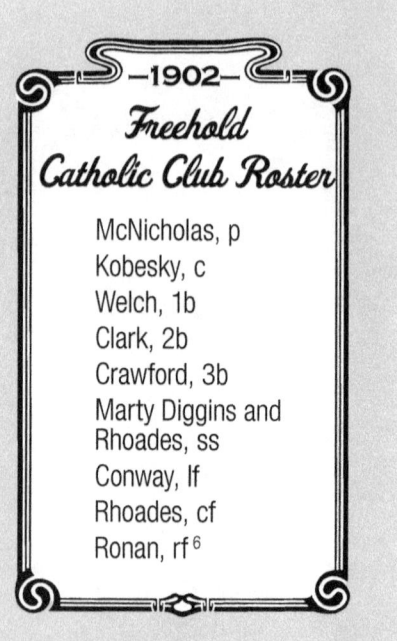

—1902—
Freehold
Catholic Club Roster

McNicholas, p
Kobesky, c
Welch, 1b
Clark, 2b
Crawford, 3b
Marty Diggins and
Rhoades, ss
Conway, lf
Rhoades, cf
Ronan, rf[6]

and his last appearances were in July. Tony and his mute team-mate, Jones, despite their "has-been" status, still managed to eke out a 16–12 victory over the Pastime A.C.s (Athletic Clubs) of Keyport.

The second game that July, however, was far from pretty. Tony stopped playing in the second inning and was replaced by Jameson. The final score was a disgraceful win for Matawan, 28–8. The Matawan fans yelled a well-deserved "You can't play marbles."[5]

Before moving to Rahway, New Jersey, my uncle, Edward C. Cashion, would manage two more teams over the next few years. In 1902, the Catholic Base Ball Club [the last time the word baseball is separated in reportage] was formed. Tony ended his playing days with this club.

On May 10, 1902, the Freehold Catholic Club would lose to the Freehold Club, 12–2. The Catholic team's new uniforms were white with "Freehold C.C." in black letters. Caps were Chicago white with black stripes. Stockings were black with white stripes and black belts.

Not Much Coverage

While the Freehold C.C. undoubtedly played some games over the next couple of years, the local reportage was skimpy at best. The only record of another game was when the Catholic Club played the Jamesburg Reform School in

These Cashion brothers were on a Freehold baseball team c. 1904. David Demarest Cashion is second from left in the center row; William Cashion is in the far left of the top row; Edward C. Cashion is in the center of the top row. Courtesy of Cashion archives

August 1904 and were beaten by a score of 13–9, and the "local players claimed they were beaten by unfair decisions on the part of the umpire."[7]

Following William Freeman, Edward C. Cashion became manager of the Freehold team before E. I. Vanderveer's much longer tenure as manager. One of my prized photos is of the local Freehold team, with Edward dressed in his managerial business attire, my father, David Demarest Cashion (1888–1941), holding his catcher's glove, and my other uncle, Bill Cashion, who played ball for a short time.

My brother, Dem Cashion, once related that his uncle had one problem during his managing days. The problem was a pitcher—a good one. According to Dem, "My uncle and

One of E. I. Vanderveer's teams circa 1904. From left to right on the front row: Fred Ely, Charles Storms, Theodore (Dory) Heyers, Edwin C. Bacon. Second row: Bobby Tyack, Sam McCue, Willard Throckmorton. Third row: Dr. Harvey Brown, Alfred Petitt, E. I. Vanderveer, Tom Richardson, Ted Beekman. Courtesy of Freehold Public Library

Edward C. Cashion (1880–1936), manager. Courtesy of Cashion archives

father would have to lock him up in his room at night to keep him sober for the next day's game."[8]

The plethora of baseball team expansion continued rapidly during the period from 1901 to 1940. Some teams lasted a few games, some lasted a couple of seasons, and the more prominent teams lasted several years. Some businesses briefly got into the baseball arena. American Steam Laundry, located at 90 Bowne Avenue, fielded a team in 1905. While only five games are recorded, the Laundrymen came out with four wins.

There is another family connection with this team. My grandmother's twin sister, Amelia Farrell, married Albert Bearmore, and he owned the business for a short time. The lineup of the team also lists a couple of Cashions.

Playing ball for different teams was common in Freehold. The players couldn't get enough baseball and would play as many days during the week as their schedules permitted. For example, on August 31, 1905, Dr.

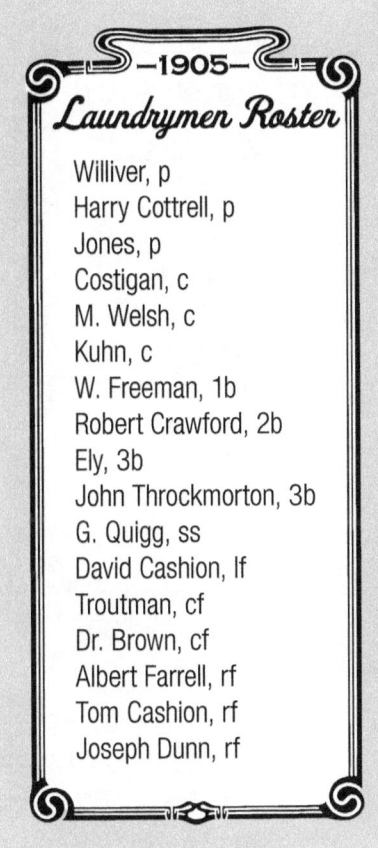

—1905—

Laundrymen Roster

Williver, p
Harry Cottrell, p
Jones, p
Costigan, c
M. Welsh, c
Kuhn, c
W. Freeman, 1b
Robert Crawford, 2b
Ely, 3b
John Throckmorton, 3b
G. Quigg, ss
David Cashion, lf
Troutman, cf
Dr. Brown, cf
Albert Farrell, rf
Tom Cashion, rf
Joseph Dunn, rf

Brown was in center field for the Freehold Seniors when they beat the American Steam Laundry team 8–3. And on October 4, 1905, he was in center field for the American Steam Laundry club when they clobbered the West Freehold team 22–10.[9] Doc Brown (1874–1944) was a practicing physician in Freehold for forty-five years and an active member of the Good Will Hook and Ladder Company; he was also the Freehold Fire Department physician for forty-three years. He played on several Freehold baseball teams.[10]

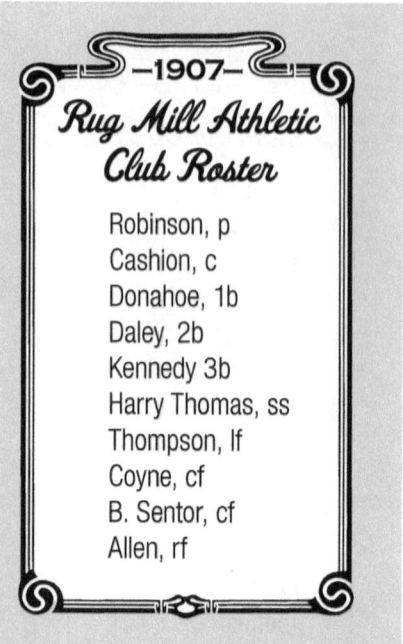

—1907—

Rug Mill Athletic Club Roster

Robinson, p
Cashion, c
Donahoe, 1b
Daley, 2b
Kennedy 3b
Harry Thomas, ss
Thompson, lf
Coyne, cf
B. Sentor, cf
Allen, rf

A. & M. Karagheusian opened its rug factory in Freehold in 1904 and for sixty years was the major employer in Freehold, at its peak employing approximately 1,700. Shortly after its opening, employees established a Rug Mill Athletic Club.[11]

The English background of many of the rug mill employees ensured that cricket was included in the Athletic Club's activities. However, they did establish a couple of baseball teams and competed with local Freehold teams during 1907. The Rug Mill team's last recorded game was in July 1933, when they beat the American Legion team 30–3.[12]

On May 4, 1912, the rug mill held a departmental ball game. The Freehold Creelers baseball team defeated the Weavers team by a score of 17–8.[13] A couple of decades later, in August 1933, the Winding Room nine beat the Designers 12–7. Then the Wash Plant All-Stars defeated the Y.M.H.A. by a score of 23–16.[14] It makes you wonder how many teams existed at the rug mill.

Girls Get in the Game

Not to be outshone, the female employees of the rug mill took to the diamond in 1940. "During the past few weeks, the baseball fans have had the pleasure of seeing young girls play the game of baseball on the diamond of the Freehold Military

School, located between Hull Avenue and Lincoln Place. The novelty has attracted many interested and some curious. The style of game is similar, but naturally played in a more restrained manner. The Messrs. Karagheusian, as an incentive, equipped the young ladies with appropriate suits upon the basis of the first game won by each. Both nines now have uniforms.

"The spirit of baseball has gripped the entire employees who are doing their bit by attendance and contributing to the freewill collection and also by purchasing for a nominal price posters for their automobiles. The families of the employees get fun and recreation out of the game."[15] Within a few years, with many rug mill men arriving home from their military service, the rug mill will sponsor one of the best ball clubs of the postwar era.

An interesting game was held in August of 1922 between the merchants of West Main Street and the merchants of East Main Street. It was a twi-

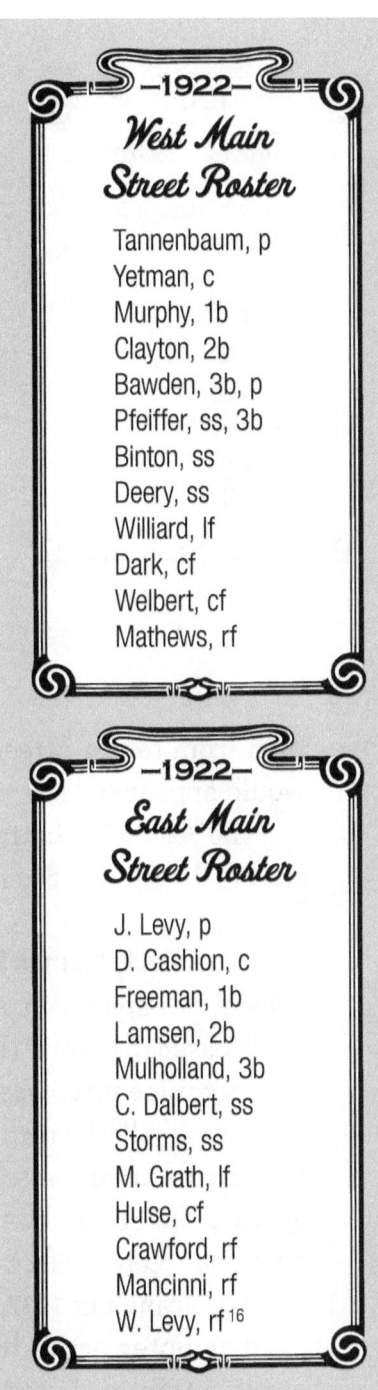

–1922–

West Main Street Roster

Tannenbaum, p
Yetman, c
Murphy, 1b
Clayton, 2b
Bawden, 3b, p
Pfeiffer, ss, 3b
Binton, ss
Deery, ss
Williard, lf
Dark, cf
Welbert, cf
Mathews, rf

–1922–

East Main Street Roster

J. Levy, p
D. Cashion, c
Freeman, 1b
Lamsen, 2b
Mulholland, 3b
C. Dalbert, ss
Storms, ss
M. Grath, lf
Hulse, cf
Crawford, rf
Mancinni, rf
W. Levy, rf[16]

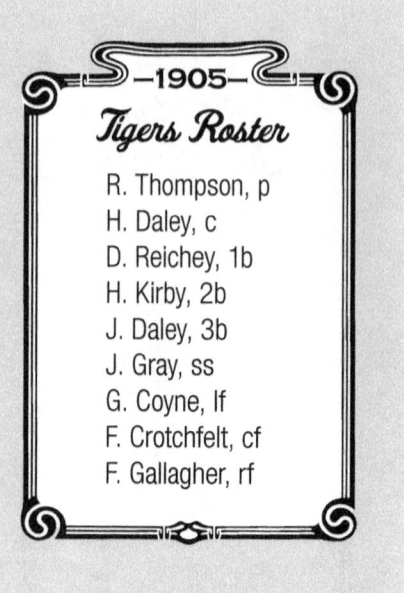

—1905—
Tigers Roster

R. Thompson, p
H. Daley, c
D. Reichey, 1b
H. Kirby, 2b
J. Daley, 3b
J. Gray, ss
G. Coyne, lf
F. Crotchfelt, cf
F. Gallagher, rf

light game, going only seven innings due to darkness. The East Main team defeated the West Main team 10–2.

"East Main Street easily solved the slants of Tannenbaum and Bawden, who pitched for the West Main team. The battery of 'Joe' Levy, the East Side motorman and 'Dem' Cashion, the old-time backstop, worked very well for the East Main Street team."

The Tigers of 1905 and the Athletics of 1913 were short-lived teams of young men from ten to fifteen years of age. Many of the players would appear in later years on various teams.

The Athletics' battery was Collins, Briggs, and Quinn. Harold Briggs was the manager of the Athletics.[17,18]

The First Black Team is Formed

A local newspaper in 1905 announced the formation of a Black baseball team: "The Colored Baseball team of Freehold will organize next week."[19] During the formative years of Black baseball, the term "colored" was used when referring to African Americans. The Colored Freehold Team played against the Freehold Athletics in 1913, the Boy Scouts in 1914, the Freehold Firemen in 1930, and the Feingold Specials in Long Branch in 1932.

It is noteworthy that "until 1947, when a new state constitution outlawed segregation in New Jersey, Black children in Freehold went to a separate grammar school from white children: the Court Street School on a small hill at the western edge of the neighborhood known as the Peach Orchard. It was originally known as the Freehold Colored School, and it started in 1915 in a small house at the foot of that hill."[20]

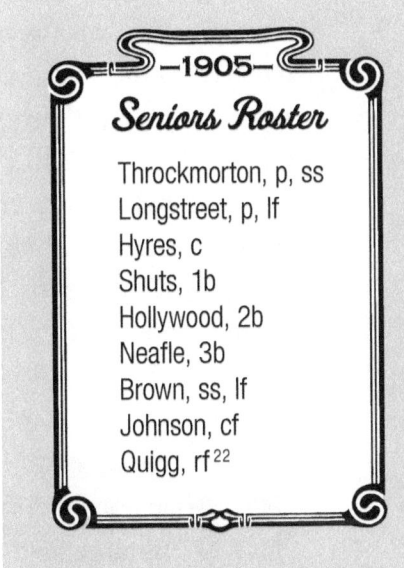

—1905—

Seniors Roster

Throckmorton, p, ss
Longstreet, p, lf
Hyres, c
Shuts, 1b
Hollywood, 2b
Neafle, 3b
Brown, ss, lf
Johnson, cf
Quigg, rf [22]

During 1904–1906, the dominant Freehold team was the Freehold Seniors, managed by E. I. Vanderveer, who would bring several championships to Freehold teams over the next thirty-plus years. On September 7, 1904, the Seniors defeated the Trenton Bowman team 2–1 in a well-played game.

"In the first inning, Edmund Parker hit a fly to left field and lost it in the grass. He came home. Longstreet and Storms, our battery, did fine work. Hyer on first held them all without a fumble. Parker on second put the visitor runners out when they tried to steal. Brown at short stopped some good ones and caught a fine fly. Throckmorton on third made good throws to first and second. Walsh in center field caught a warm liner. Quigg at right field and Ely in left were not bothered by fly balls as the visitors were unable to get 'Ding's' twirlers out of the diamond."[21]

Edward Cashion served as the Freehold Seniors' secretary in 1904 and was responsible for scheduling their fifty-game season.

In 1905, the Seniors played a doubleheader in two different towns on Decoration Day. In the morning, they played the Princeton A.C. club on the Broadway grounds in Freehold and beat them 7-6. In the afternoon, they went to Long Branch and beat a top-rated team by a score of 6-3. Longstreet twirled a great game in the afternoon, allowing only three hits and striking out eleven.

The Seniors had another long season in 1905. Some of the scheduled games were as follows:

MAY 6–Nationals of Perth Amboy, at Freehold
MAY 13–Brandons of New York, at Freehold
MAY 20–Chiltons of Elizabeth, at Freehold
MAY 30–Carteret Field Club, at Freehold
JUNE 3–Yorkville B.B. Club, at Freehold
JULY 8–Park A.C. of Newark, at Freehold
JULY 22–Freehold at Asbury Park
AUGUST 19–West Side A.C. of Jersey City, at Freehold
SEPTEMBER 4–All-Star A.C. of Newark, two games
               at Freehold
SEPTEMBER 30–Chester A.C. of Newark, at Freehold[23]

One of the games added to the Seniors' schedule was on September 12, 1905, when they played the Brooklyn Royal Giants. The Giants were a formidable foe for over two decades. While the Freehold Seniors lost the game 6-4, the local team played well.

"The feature of the game was the playing of Edwards on third, he making several sensational catches and throws to first base. Longstreet (Ding) in the box was at his best, keeping a number of the crack players from reaching first base."[24]

The Freehold Seniors' 1905 season ended with a record of 22 wins, 15 losses.[25]

My Dad Was in It for the Long Haul

My father, David Demarest Cashion, played baseball for about fifteen years and umpired for another eighteen years. He began playing in 1904, joined the American Steam Laundry team in 1905, the rug mill team in 1907 and played with the Freehold team until 1919. In

My father, David Demarest Cashion (1888–1941), had notoriety as both a catcher and an umpire. Courtesy of Cashion archives

the early years, Cashion's brother Edward was the manager, and his other brother, William, served as the secretary.

Cashion became an outstanding catcher and from 1908 to 1919 was a standout player. When he wasn't catching, he would play in the outfield (to keep his bat in the lineup). The Freehold club played teams throughout the region, including Elizabeth, Point Pleasant, Long Branch, and Bay Head.

In 1910, Freehold was matched against the Philadelphia Colored Giants, said to be the fastest colored team in the world.[27] The Philadelphia Giants competed from 1902 to 1911. They were known as one of the strongest teams in Black baseball, winning five eastern championships in six

The Philadelphia Colored Giants, c. 1905. From left to right on the front row: Bill Monroe, Pete Booker. Second row: Home Run Johnson, Charlie Grant, Walter Schlichter, Rube Foster, Pete Hill. Third row: Harry Smith, Henry W. Moore, Emmett Bowman, Sol White, Tom Washington, Dan McClellan. Courtesy of Wikimedia Commons

years.[27] In a closely contested game, the Giants defeated the Freehold team 2–0.

In 1916, at a meeting held at the Wolcott house, Cashion was elected manager of the Freehold team. The team also agreed to improve the Broadway grounds and erect a grandstand. Cashion announced that he had secured the services of two outstanding recruits and was confident of a very successful season.[28]

Indeed, the Freehold team went on to win the championship that year. Cashion also coached the Freehold High School Varsity baseball team in 1919. Several familiar Freehold names were on that team: Herman Stokes, Fred

Ed King (first row, second from right) played for the 1922 Freehold High School team and was also a star pitcher of the Freehold Firemen. Courtesy of Monmouth County Historical Association

Quinn, Joe Laird, Alvah Vanderveer, Bill Willet, Walter and Gilday Freeman, Harold Holmes, and Ed King.[29]

While Cashion's active participation as a baseball player ended around 1919, his interest in baseball continued unabated. He became a baseball umpire in 1920 and was a beloved and respected umpire for the next eighteen years. The earliest recorded game with Cashion behind the plate was July 5, 1920, with the Freehold baseball team taking two games from Princeton A.C. at the Lincoln Street field in Freehold. Four hundred people witnessed both games.[30]

The Freehold club continued their winning ways in 1921, and Cashion was the umpire-in-chief for most of the games.

The town's enthusiasm for baseball was never more in evidence than on July 17, 1921, when Freehold won a doubleheader over the Kent All-Stars of Newark and the Newark American Legion team. Attendance at this doubleheader was 1,500 at the Lincoln Street field.[31]

Cashion's umpiring skills and general demeanor with the teams afforded him a great deal of notoriety throughout Central New Jersey baseball leagues. In 1921, a reporter noted, "He knows the rules and inside baseball, and keeps his eagle eyes on the ball."[32] Following a game between prep schools in 1922, a reporter stated: "Dem is proving a fine fellow with the younger students."[33] In 1923, after a Princeton University game, "Dem's umpiring was faultless, and Dem made a good impression upon the student body."[34]

This year also marked another colossal attendance of 1,500 at the Lincoln Street field, as Freehold knocked off the Bordentown team, champions of the Burlington County league, and Cashion called balls and strikes.[35] He became known throughout Central New Jersey for his umpiring skills and gregarious nature. By 1926, Cashion had reached a plateau of umpiring excellence, and the Jersey Shore Umpire Organization asked him to umpire the game of his life.

On October 10, 1926, the New York Yankees lost the World Series to the St. Louis Cardinals in a hotly contested seven-game series. Babe Ruth embarked immediately afterward on a whirlwind barnstorming tour, including nine cities in sixteen days. On October 11, 1926, Babe Ruth and his All-Star baseball team held their first exhibition game at Bradley Beach, New Jersey. The game pitted the Yankee All-Star team against the Royal Giants of Brooklyn.[36] Cashion's well-known skills earned him the opportunity to umpire behind the plate at this noteworthy game.

My dad, David Cashion, umpired behind the plate in Babe Ruth's barnstorming game in Bradley Beach in 1926. Courtesy of Cashion archives

The town of Bradley Beach enthusiastically supported this game. It was the largest crowd that had ever attended a game at the Bradley Beach field. Local newspaper accounts and *New York Times* reporting had the size of the crowd at 3,500–5,000.[37]

Babe's first appearance at bat resulted in a soft grounder to the pitcher for an easy out. The crowd was hoping for a greater display of power from the mighty Babe. At his next appearance at the plate, Babe watched a couple of wild pitches go by and also fouled off two pitches. He then watched a pitch be called a strike, and Cashion called him out.

At his next two plate appearances, Babe did meet the crowd's expectations by belting balls over the temporary fence for ground-rule doubles. Ruth's All-Stars lost to the Royal Giants by the score of 3–1. The local newspaper reported that "Cashion behind the home plate umpired the game in a creditable manner."[38]

Many years later, in 1938, Cashion stopped by the Freehold Courthouse to chat with some friends. In a group conversation, attorney Isidore Friedman brought up the famous Bradley Beach baseball game in which Cashion had called out the then home run king on three strikes. Cashion responded that Babe had turned around slowly and remarked, "Well, I guess you're right."[39] A photo of my father behind home plate at the Bradley Beach game remained on my mother's dresser throughout her life.

The Sin of Sunday Baseball

From the 1850s, when baseball started in Freehold, games were not allowed to be played on Sundays. In 1884, the Monmouth Democrat urged "that measures be taken to stop the evil. This is another Sunday nuisance."[40] In 1889, laws were proposed "to make Sunday baseball a misdemeanor, punishable by a fine of $30 or thirty days imprisonment, or both."[41] In 1908, the Monmouth County church officials issued a resolution stating, "Sunday baseball . . . brings with it the attendant evils of the demoralization of the young, the serious violation of the Holy Sabbath, together with drinking, betting and fighting."[42] They urged all ministers, editors of local papers, and all public officials to raise a public sentiment that would speedily eradicate this evil.

The general public was not against Sunday baseball; however, it took several years of grassroots efforts to legalize it. Games were played on Sunday at the Lincoln Place field, but they were played contrary to law. Finally, in 1921, a petition signed by one thousand voters was offered to the court in support of the continuance of Sunday baseball. The petition stated that the crowds attending the games were law-abiding and that the best interests of the community demanded Sunday afternoon baseball games.

E. I. Vanderveer, manager of the Lincoln Place field, and attorney Joseph McDermott spearheaded the drive for Sunday baseball. Supporting affidavits stated that Sunday games were orderly and that the only noise in the neighborhood was caused by handclapping, which only lasted for a few minutes. These affidavits were submitted by Mrs. James Frost, Mrs. Frank Sickles, and my grandmother, Mrs. Jennie McNicholas.[43]

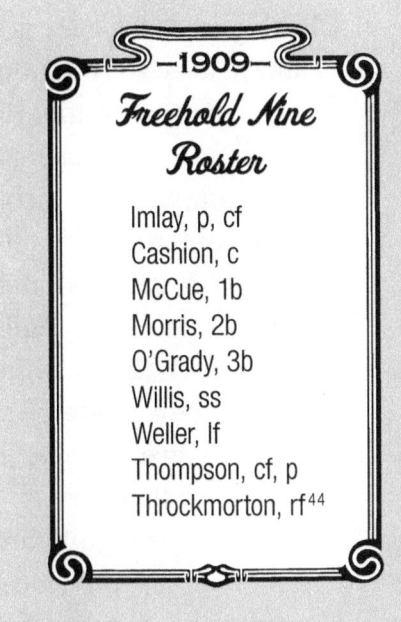

–1909–
Freehold Nine Roster

Imlay, p, cf
Cashion, c
McCue, 1b
Morris, 2b
O'Grady, 3b
Willis, ss
Weller, lf
Thompson, cf, p
Throckmorton, rf[44]

For about thirty years, starting in 1906, there was a baseball team called "Freehold." At times, it was simply Freehold; other times, it was Freehold A.C. And for a while it was known as Freehold Baseball Club (Freehold B.B.C.). For an inexplicable reason, there was a lapse of four years from 1928 to 1932, until Vanderveer retook the managerial reins.

Many of the teams during those thirty years were outstanding. During that time, attendance at games skyrocketed. Several ball fields were used, including Broadway, Manalapan Avenue, Jerseyville Avenue, Lincoln Place, Monument Park, and the Freehold Driving Park, using the inner area of the raceway.

During the first decade of the Freehold nine, the team went through interesting times. They had their moments in the sun, but those were few and far between. For example, in August 1909, they trounced Trenton 15–6. In the same month, they were shut out by Asbury Park 2–0 and 3–2.

In 1906 at a meeting in Red Bank, the Monmouth County Baseball League was formed. Representatives from Red Bank, Long Branch, Atlantic Highlands, Asbury Park, Matawan, and Freehold agreed to establish this league. A formal constitution and by-laws were drawn up and officers were elected. Benjamin Ford, Red Bank, was named president; William Joline, Long Branch, was vice president, and William Bedle of Matawan was secretary and treasurer. My great uncle, Jim Fitzgibbon, was named the Red Bank representative.

The most significant element of this new league was that it was a professional league. "The visiting teams shall receive forty percent of the gate receipts and the home team sixty percent of all the games. It was proposed to buy a $25 or $30 pennant to be given to the team with the highest average at the end of the season. In February 1907, the pennant for the 1906 year was officially awarded to Red Bank."[45]

Of interest, it was noted in a local newspaper in 1906 that a baseball thrown by a professional player with a good arm goes at the rate of about eighty miles per hour. One wonders if our Freehold hurlers were able to deliver at that speed.[46]

The Freehold fans truly appreciated the Freehold team. The first recorded attendance was in September 1906, with three hundred at the Broadway grounds. Spectator interest would increase dramatically over the next couple of decades. My father would continue to play and be recognized for his playing ability.

"Inmay and Cashion was the Freehold battery and played in their easy form."[47] "Dem Cashion, Freehold's catcher, injured his finger in one of the Asbury Park games last week, and it was a very sore Saturday, but he stood up through the whole game and did not drop the ball once when it counted for anything."[48]

Freehold's first night game under the lights was played on July 9, 1910, on the Broadway grounds, against the Cherokee Indians traveling baseball team. The Indians toured the country and brought fifty incandescent arc lights and their own band. The ball used in the evening game was a little larger than the one used in an ordinary game, being ten inches in circumference.

Also during this decade, the two military schools, the New Jersey Military Academy and the Freehold Military School, played in a Triangle League with the local high school. Additionally, the Freehold Nationals was a team of youngsters that evolved into a YMCA team and played under that banner for a couple of years.

As the next few years unfold, Freehold develops a championship team that absolutely dominates all competition. Attendance booms as a result. The emergence of integrated teams is also on the horizon.

Chapter 4

1916-1937: RECORD-BREAKING CROWDS

*"People ask me what do I do when there's no baseball.
I'll tell you what I do. I stare out the
window and wait for spring."*
—ROGER HORNSBY

The decade of 1916-1926 is exciting because it's when fans started gathering around radios to listen attentively to games. We will also meet the grandfather of Freehold baseball, E. I. Vanderveer. And we will learn how one player bravely gathered intelligence for the U.S. military while on a team trip to Japan.

On July 5, 1920, the Freehold baseball team played a doubleheader on the Lincoln Street diamond with the Princeton Athletic Club's nine. The crowd, estimated at four hundred, witnessed a cleanly played game. Freehold won both games (4–2 and 15–7), with heavy hitter Mutt Meyers driving out a homer.

This game marked the first time my father left behind the "tools of ignorance" and donned the umpire's uniform.

Baseball fans gave evidence of their appreciation of the local ball club by holding a banquet for the team on October 18,

One of E. I. Vanderveer's winning teams: Freehold 1920. From left to right on the front row: Thomson, Carswell, Williams, Daly, Rue, Boyle. Back row: Hines, E. I. Vanderveer, Meyers, Briggs, Cashion, W. Halderman, Quinn, Kennedy. Courtesy of Michael Wilson collection

1920, at the Monmouth House. A duck dinner was served with all the trimmings. A local orchestra provided music, and all had a grand time.

The attendee list was a "who's who" of Freehold baseball: E. I. Vanderveer (organizer), Walter Kennedy (manager), Dem Cashion (their ever-faithful umpire), Alvah Vanderveer, Rensen Meyers, Gene Williams, Fred Quinn, Joseph Boyle, Robert Thompson, Harry Daley, William

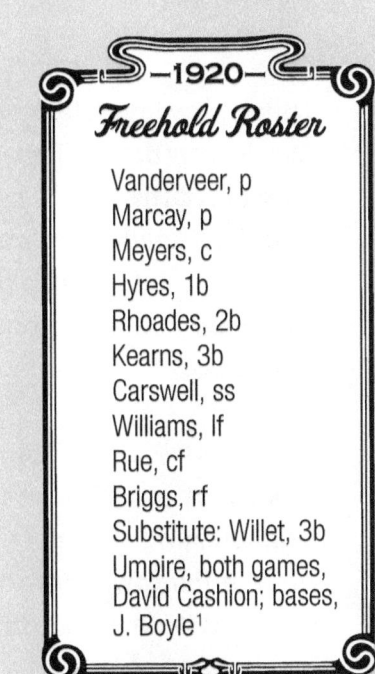

–1920–
Freehold Roster

Vanderveer, p
Marcay, p
Meyers, c
Hyres, 1b
Rhoades, 2b
Kearns, 3b
Carswell, ss
Williams, lf
Rue, cf
Briggs, rf
Substitute: Willet, 3b
Umpire, both games,
David Cashion; bases,
J. Boyle[1]

The 1922 Freehold team included (top row) E. I. Vanderveer (fourth from left), Alvah "Oodles" Vanderveer (third from right), and my dad, David Cashion (far right). Courtesy of Cashion archives

Willett, Ray Jones, Joseph Hardiman, James Kearns Jr., Horace Rue, Walter Briggs, James Booth, John Carswell, and the two mascots of the team, Francis Mitchell and Sherwen Benton. William Rhoades was unable to attend due to a death in the family. Miniature bats that were filled with candy and tied with blue and gold ribbon (the club's colors) were given as souvenirs.[2]

Fans Adore Winning Team

From 1921 to 1926, the Freehold nine were practically unbeatable, and the spectators turned out in droves to view their hometown heroes. Due to scheduling snafus, *two* teams showed up on the Lincoln Place field to play against Freehold's club on July 15, 1921.

In the first game, the Kent All-Stars of Newark were defeated 7–6, behind the pitching of Alvah "Oodles" Vanderveer and the hitting of Rhoades and Meyers. In the second game, Vanderveer was again the hurler and pitched a beautiful four-hitter, and Freehold won 7–0. Cashion was the umpire, as usual. And the attendance was reported at 1,500, which was 33 percent of Freehold's population at the time.[3]

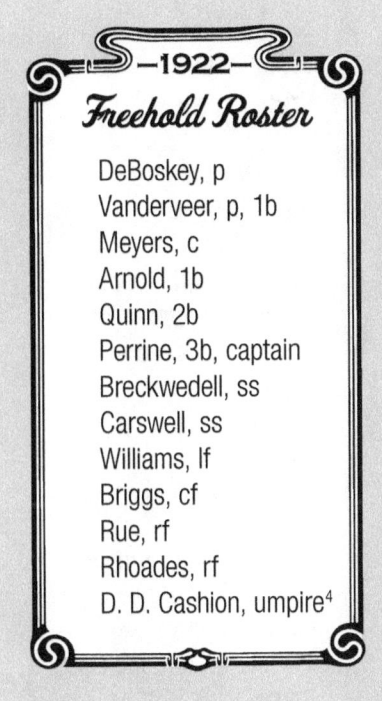

–1922–

Freehold Roster

DeBoskey, p
Vanderveer, p, 1b
Meyers, c
Arnold, 1b
Quinn, 2b
Perrine, 3b, captain
Breckwedell, ss
Carswell, ss
Williams, lf
Briggs, cf
Rue, rf
Rhoades, rf
D. D. Cashion, umpire[4]

The Freehold club was part of the Three-M League in 1922 and 1923. The league consisted of Freehold, Bash A.C. (Athletic Club), Yardville, Hightstown, Cranbury, and Lakewood. Freehold won the Three-M League championship in 1922. Freehold claimed the title; however, the league's governing committee decided that Freehold would have to win two out of three more with Yardville to truly be declared winners. Manager Vanderveer stated that Freehold had won it once and did not intend to win it again, so the additional games were not played.

At midyear 1923, the Freehold team was "on fire." By July 1, they had won twenty-two of twenty-seven games, and Gene Williams was leading the team in batting with a .418 average. The local media was actually growing disenchanted with the team's success. "Discriminating fans declare

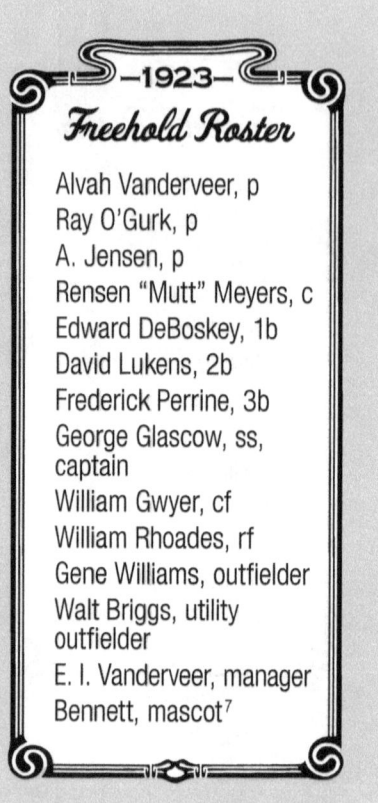

—1923—
Freehold Roster

Alvah Vanderveer, p
Ray O'Gurk, p
A. Jensen, p
Rensen "Mutt" Meyers, c
Edward DeBoskey, 1b
David Lukens, 2b
Frederick Perrine, 3b
George Glascow, ss, captain
William Gwyer, cf
William Rhoades, rf
Gene Williams, outfielder
Walt Briggs, utility outfielder
E. I. Vanderveer, manager
Bennett, mascot[7]

that the games are too one-sided and that teams of better players should be sought."[5]

The local nine, however, did not let up. They went on to win the Monmouth County Championship with a record of 45–16. On July 1, Freehold beat Bordentown 8–5 behind the pitching of Jensen, brought to the team from Perth Amboy by Manager Vanderveer.

The attendance at this game was again 1,500.[6]

In the show window of Vanderveer's office on East Main Street, two cups were proudly displayed starting in 1924. One was donated to the Freehold baseball club by County Clerk Joseph McDermott for winning the 1922 Three-M League championship. The other was donated to the Freehold team by Louis B. Tim, president of the Norwood Field club of Long Branch, for winning the Monmouth County baseball championship for the 1923 season.[8]

Gene Williams managed the 1924 Freehold team. Williams acquired a couple of stellar new players and hoped for another championship year. They played their games at the Freehold Driving Park grounds, and a grandstand was now available for the fans. An early-season game against

Rider College, on the Broadway grounds, saw Eddie King, a recent graduate of Freehold High School and later star pitcher for the Freehold Firemen's team, pitch against Freehold. The team ended the season with a record of 30–17; however, it was not good enough to win the title.

Two games to highlight from the 1924 season were a home game on May 22, 1924, and an away game at Bradley Beach on August 2, 1924. Freehold was pitted against the Colored Giants of Philadelphia in the May game. A large number of fans expected to see a closely fought contest. Instead, the visitors were completely outclassed, and Freehold defeated the usually sharp team 16–0.[9]

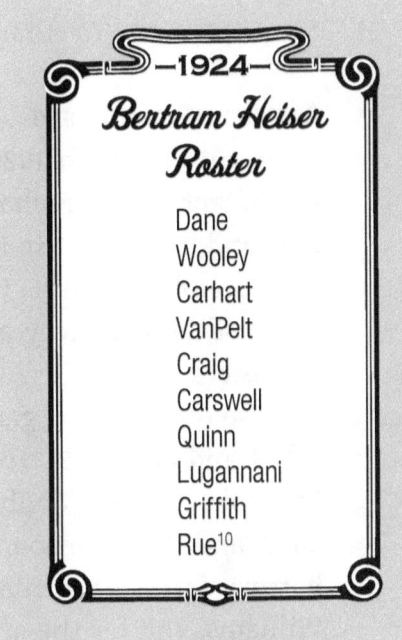

—1924—
Bertram Heiser Roster

Dane
Wooley
Carhart
VanPelt
Craig
Carswell
Quinn
Lugannani
Griffith
Rue[10]

It is worth noting that at this point in the season, Freehold's record was twenty-five wins and four losses.

At the Bradly Beach game, with two thousand fans in attendance, Freehold ran up a big win by the score of 13–3. Ed DeBoskey and Gene Williams contributed three hits apiece and drove in eight of the thirteen runs.

Bertram Heiser organized another amateur team of Freehold and Matawan players in 1924.

While this team did not last, Quinn and Lugannani would later become stars of the Freehold Firemen team. This time frame brought forth a plethora of start-up teams with limited duration, such as the Meadowbrooks, the Single Men, the West End, the Red Men, and the Foresters.

Awesome Black Teams

From 1916 through 1929, two Black baseball teams were prominent on the Freehold diamonds. The Excelsior A.C. was one, and it lost 10–1 to Freehold at the Broadway grounds on September 16, 1916. Hendrickson and Cashion were the Freehold club's battery, and Layton and Little served for the Excelsiors.[11]

Two other strong games by the Excelsiors occurred on July 1 and July 8, 1917. On July 1st, they clearly outclassed Freehold A.C. in a doubleheader. The morning score was 28–2, and the afternoon score was 30–3.[12] The Excelsiors' battery for the morning game was Al Jones and James Williams, and for the afternoon game, Charlies Jones and James Williams.

On July 8th, Brown pitched and Jones and Williams caught for the Excelsiors as they defeated Farmingdale 14–12.[13] On Decoration Day 1919, the local news report noted, "The local colored boys Excelsiors have a fast baseball nine. They swamped the Rug Mill Nine, on the Broadway ground, 13–3. J. Henderson and Elmer Jackson held the Rug Mill boys to two hits."[14]

The second stellar Black baseball club from 1928 to 1929 was the 40 A.C. This team was in the same league with the Freehold Firemen, the Englishtown Firemen, Highlands A.C., and Lakewood. The 40 A.C. battery alternated between Bergen and Hutchins and Hank Schanck and Hutchins.[15]

Hank Schanck would continue as a baseball star in Freehold and was one of the first Black people to play for the town's elite white ball clubs. Schanck lived a few doors

Hank Schanck, one of the first African American ball players in Freehold, was a great athlete. Courtesy of Roberta Schanck

down the street from the Lincoln Place field and loved the game of baseball. He was a teammate of my brother Dem (same nickname as my father) on the 1937 championship National Lead baseball team. He started in the infield and evolved into an outstanding pitcher. He then played for the Freehold Holy Name team during its peak seasons and joined the Freehold Gulistans in 1938.

Both Schanck and Cashion worked at National Lead Industries in Perth Amboy, and both played for the National Lead team in the Industrial League of Middlesex County, a top-caliber league. They played for National Lead during the week, allowing them to play for Freehold Holy Name (FHN) on Sundays. Cashion led the National Lead nine to first place in the Industrial League. A newspaper of that locality shows Cashion "a dependable hurler and handler of a wicked bat."[16]

My memory of Schanck was his dominant presence as an umpire during my playing days. At that time I had no inkling that he and my brother had been teammates in the late 1930s and 1940s. I do remember that Schanck was definitely in control of the game while umpiring.

Schanck's dedication to baseball was clearly in evidence on the day his daughter was born in 1937. Schanck's wife, Mabel, suddenly went into labor and there was not enough time to get her to Fitkin Hospital in Neptune, which was a half hour from Freehold. Fortunately, the original Freehold Hospital on West Main Street was available. Hank and Mabel rushed to Dr. Reynolds at the hospital, where Roberta was delivered safely. Schanck was present during the delivery, and when he saw his new daughter he stood tall and proud—in his baseball uniform.

The Freehold Baseball Club bounced back into the winning circle in 1925. On November 15, 1925, at the Freehold Driving Association Park, Freehold defeated the Norwoods of Long Branch 7–2 and won its second Monmouth County Championship in three years. The estimated attendance at this game was one thousand.

For this season, Vanderveer brought in several players from other leagues, and he orchestrated quite a formidable team.

Also during this season, the Freehold fans flocked to the games at the interior area of the Freehold Racetrack, with its newly erected grandstand. The attendance records were as follows: 1,400 on May 17, 1925, as Freehold nipped the Newark Pros 3–2; they lost a close one to the Newark Pros on June 14, 1925, before 1,100 fans, and they lost to a rugged Bradley Beach nine in June 1925, with an attendance of 1,200.

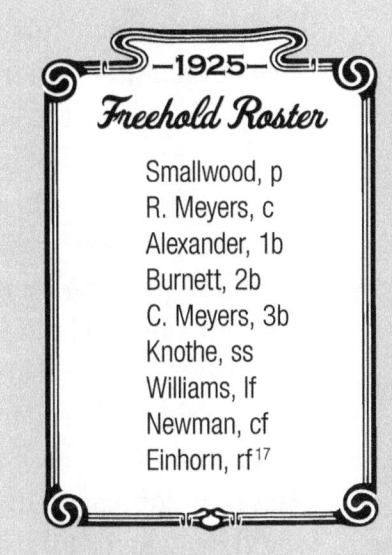

–1925–
Freehold Roster

Smallwood, p
R. Meyers, c
Alexander, 1b
Burnett, 2b
C. Meyers, 3b
Knothe, ss
Williams, lf
Newman, cf
Einhorn, rf[17]

Vanderveer fielded his 1926 team with a return of his local ball players: his son Oodles Vanderveer, Lugannani, and Eddie King on the mound; "Mutt" Meyers behind the plate; and Briggs, Carswell, Eskew, Quinn, Gene Williams, Herbert, and Billy Rhoades.

In 1932, the Freehold team acquired a young Frankie Hayes from Jamesburg to play in the outfield. On September 12, 1932, the Freehold team defeated the Colored House of David 8–3. The Colored House of David team was managed by Harry Crump. The team played in small towns across the country and featured former Negro League stars such as "Rocking Chair Catcher" 'Babe' McCray, "Cannonball" Berry, and "Flier" Coleman.[18]

A Crazy Year

The 1933 Freehold Baseball Club season was a topsy-turvy year. At the start of the season, a new entrant emerged on the baseball horizon: Philadelphian Frank Magnifico, who managed the team at the beginning of the season. He brought some new talent to the club while retaining some of the Freehold regulars, including young Frankie Hayes. The team took on a new name, the Pirates, and played several games under that banner, including games against the Cuban All-Stars and the Baltimore Black Sox. Unfortunately, Magnifico ran into player issues and financial issues.

By July, Vanderveer had taken over the team and renamed it the Freehold Baseball Club. Strangely, Magnifico returned to Freehold and took over the team again, bringing back the Pirates name. Magnifico said he had to repay some debts. Plus, he had grand aspirations of creating a Class D minor league in the Central New Jersey area, which would include his Pirate team.[19]

Not to be outdone by this turn of events, Vanderveer resurrected his Freehold nine, and a grudge three-game series was held in September between the Pirates and the Freehold Baseball Club. Freehold won the first game of the series; the second resulted in a twelve-inning tie. In the final game, the Freehold team was victorious 10–1.

Tempers were at a fever pitch during this final game. In the sixth inning, King, the Pirate catcher, grumbled all along about calls made by the umpire, Cashion. In King's last at bat, Cashion called him out on strikes. "As he was donning his catching paraphernalia, King was heard to make some remarks. Cashion took exception to one of King's remarks, and before anyone knew anything, umpire Cashion and King were in a clinch . . . and hands were flying."[20] Things finally settled down, but this was the Pirates' last hurrah in Freehold.

The last recorded season of the Freehold club was 1934. They ended with a very respectable record of twenty-six wins and three losses.[21]

Freehold's baseball enthusiasm extended well beyond their local heroes. They read any narrative and box score of the professional baseball leagues with great interest. Naturally, during World Series time, their interest soared. In 1924, the New York Giants and the Washington Senators were in the World Series.

The town's residents were able to hear the play-by-play broadcast via a newly invented Neutrodyne radio receiver, installed on the outside of the Givens and Dubois Drug Store in the courthouse square. Using a high-power amplifier, the broadcast could be heard all over the square. Local Louis Colaner was the mastermind behind the installation.

1926 pennant-winning Knights of Columbus team. From left to right on the front row: Marty Diggins, unknown player, Gilday Freeman, Bill Rhodes, Hank Coyne. Second row: Con Clancy, Jack Queeny, Slats Carey, Raymond Sheehan, Al Daly. Third row: Joe Kennedy, Father E. S. Heil, Vince Foy. Courtesy of Kevin Coyne collection

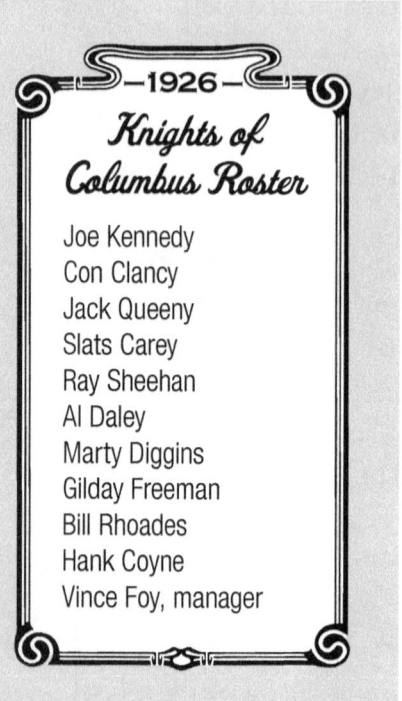

Likewise, Cliff Conners and Charles Miller operated a loudspeaker system for a crowd of baseball fans in 1925 to hear the Pittsburgh Pirates battle the Washington Senators.[22]

In 1929, at C. H. Roberson's, 26 Court Street, you could purchase baseballs that ranged in price from twenty cents to $1.75; baseball bats from fifty cents to $1.75; Wilson basemen's mitts for $2.25, and Wilson fielder's mitts for $2.25.[23]

From 1926 through the early 1930s, the Freehold Knights of Columbus fielded a talented baseball team. They had a limited number of games per season but played very well. In 1926, their first year of operation, they won the pennant, winning eight out of nine games. They beat out an excellent Colonials team, and the Foresters came in third.[24]

The last recorded Knights of Columbus game was May 24, 1931, when they beat the Bristol Knights of Columbus 21–8 on the Lincoln Place ball grounds.[25]

The Many Adventures of Edgar I. Vanderveer

E. I. Vanderveer (1870–1955) held numerous political offices during his lifetime, including coroner, township collector, postmaster, assemblyman, clerk of elections, and supervisor of transfer and inheritance taxes. He was chief of the local

E. I. Vanderveer, sans his distinguished mustache. Courtesy of Cashion archives

fire department and chairman of the executive committee of the Republican County Committee for seventeen years. He was also a director and charter member of the Freehold Trust Company. He was on championship gun teams and held several shooting records. One of his fondest memories was when he topped the famous Annie Oakley in 1916.

But with all of his notoriety, Vanderveer is best known as the "Grandfather of Freehold Baseball." There are photos of him on baseball teams as early as 1897. He quickly moved into the managerial ranks and from 1904 to 1934, Vanderveer was acknowledged as the best baseball manager in Monmouth County. He managed the last year of the Freehold Firemen team in 1938. His 1923 and 1924 teams were crowned Monmouth County champions and 3-M champions. The 3-M League was composed of semipro teams from Monmouth, Mercer, and Middlesex counties.

Vanderveer believed that the 1924 club was his greatest crew. This team consisted of his son, Oodles Vanderveer; George Glasco, the best shortstop in the state; Gene Williams, the best outfielder; "Mutt" Meyers; Ray O'Gurk; "Chubby" Perrine; "Pug" Lucas; Ed DeBoskey; Dick Newman; Bill Rhoades; and Walt Briggs.

Vanderveer stated that he'd never forget "when Bill Rhoades knocked out a homer off of Satchel Paige," a veteran of the Negro Leagues who went on to play for the St. Louis Browns, Cleveland Indians, and Kansas City Athletics.[26] As a fitting end to his managerial career, Vanderveer was selected to manage the 1934 Monmouth County All-Star team when they played the Belmar Braves. Freehold's representatives on that team were Jack Clevenger, William Haberman, Al Sabo, Oodles Vanderveer, Henny Dane, Artie Manuel, and Tom Dietz.[27]

Vanderveer continued to follow baseball and be involved long after his managerial days were over. By the time I was playing in the Freehold Little Bigger League in 1953, Vanderveer was our league commissioner.

The start of the 1925 season brought another new entrant to the Freehold baseball arena. S. L. Wood, a South Street druggist, organized a new team composed wholly of Freehold youths. Wood most likely saw a tremendous interest in baseball following the success of Vanderveer's championship teams and decided the town would benefit from a team of young men around eighteen years old who would compete against teams of players about the same age from other towns.

The new team would also play against the local teams. He called the new team the Colonials. They played on the Freehold Driving Association's grounds on Saturdays and charged a small admission fee for fans over twelve years of age. Fred Quinn was the manager, and Horace Rue was the secretary and treasurer.

The Colonials fielded a good ball club in 1925. Doc Wood's team, behind the pitching of Givens and the hitting of Kelly, with two triples, defeated Lakewood 10–7 on May 1, 1925. On Independence Day, a doubleheader was held at the Jerseyville grounds, where Barkalow pitched a winning game against Farmingdale A.C. (11–2), and Willet hurled the winning game against Trenton (5–4).[29]

The Colonials' playing days lasted through the 1928 season. In their successful 1926 season, "Lefty" Daley was the key pitcher. Playing on the Lincoln Place grounds in September of 1926, Daley held the Monmouth Beach nine to three hits and struck out eighteen batters. "During the last 45 innings that Daley has twirled, he has allowed but one earned tally in a Colonial uniform."[30]

–1925–
Colonials Roster

Lugannani or Russell, p
Kelly or Kehs, c
Egan, 1b
Morris, 2b
McGackin, 3b
Hyres, ss
Barkalow, lf
Carey, cf
Quinn, rf
Substitutes: Van-Schoick, Friedman, Givens, and Daley[28]

As with all the Freehold teams, funding was difficult. The Colonials were constantly improvising fundraising initiatives to support the team. For example, on May 18, 1925, at the United Theatre, Buster Keaton's *Seven Chances* was shown to benefit the team. Admission was twenty-five cents for the matinee and fifty cents for the evening performances. On January 17, 1927, a dance was held at St. Peter's Parish Hall. And on February 15, 1928, a dance was held in Snider's Hall on West Main Street, with the proceeds going to the purchase of new uniforms for the team.[31]

Firemen Team: One of the Best

Freehold boasted fifty-plus baseball teams from 1856 to 1972. However, the Freehold Firemen stands out among them all. The team was in operation for sixteen years and won five Firemen League championships (1930, 1931, 1932, 1935, and 1936) and two Monmouth County championships (1932 and 1935). No other team can claim that sustainability or that league prominence.

Over those sixteen years, thousands of spectators watched some very outstanding Firemen ball players. Starting in 1923 with relatively small crowds of four hundred at the Lincoln Place grounds, the Firemen defeated the Marlboro A.C.s 9–8.[32] In 1924, Rhoades and Clancy formed the battery. In an August game, the Firemen succumbed to the Englishtown team 9–2.[33] One of the significant strengths of the Freehold Firemen team during its entire sixteen-year life span was the adroit management of Joe Crotchfelt. His managerial skill, coupled with some genuinely outstanding ball players, made the Freehold Firemen a team to be feared in Monmouth County.

The Firemen team played a lot of baseball. For example, in 1926 they had a five-game series against the Englishtown fire department, starting on June 17 and ending on July 1. The local team came out on the losing side of the series.

The year 1926 also saw Eddie King join the Firemen, and he went on to become a very reliable pitcher. On June 9, 1927, King hurled a winning game against Doc Wood's Colonial team (7–6).

Most of the Firemen's games were twilight games. Noted in a July 1930 article: "Twilight baseball was quite popular at the Lincoln Street diamond. The townsmen take advantage and spend a pleasant outdoor two hours. The majority of players are old-timers, such

–1926–

Firemen Roster

E. King, p
C. Patten, c
L. Clayton, 1b
A. Vanderveer, 2b
F. Quinn, 3b
J. Carswell, ss
W. Briggs, cf
C. Daley, rf
substitutes: E. Woolfenden, C. Clancy, Stanley Keener, C. Collins, R. Connors, Leo Dugan, and H. J. Whitman[34]

as Rhoades, Vanderveer, Lugannani, Carswell, Briggs, and Quinn. They have been playing fast, clean ball, considering that the majority of them are no longer single men. There will be many twilight games during the Summer. The games are played after supper. Attending them will aid digestion."[35]

The championship seasons of 1930–1932 were powered by the pitching of Fred Quinn, Eddie King, and Charlie Lugannani and the hitting prowess of Oodles Vanderveer and Bill Rhoades. Fort Monmouth, a perennial nemesis of Freehold, won the 1933 Firemen's League championship.

The County Firemen's Baseball League trophy cup for 1931 and 1932 was presented to fifty baseball club members and guests at a lavish banquet at the Country Inn on January 31,

This is the Freehold Firemen's 1931 championship trophy. Courtesy of Nolan Higgins

1933. Major Charles Duncan and County Clerk Joseph McDermott gave short addresses. Vanderveer was in attendance, as was manager Joseph Crotchfelt and captain Bill Rhoades. "The gentlemen then gathered around the piano and furnished their own entertainment."[36]

The Firemen finally acquired a home field in 1934. They leased a plot of several acres on Manalapan Avenue, opposite the former Brakeley's Canning Factory. The season was marked with top-notch playing by the Firemen, right down to the end of the season.

An All-Star Firemen's team played against the Belmar Baseball Club in Belmar on August 19, 1934. Fred Quinn and Charlie Lugannani shared the pitching duties and brought home a 6–4 victory.[37] The season ended with the Freehold Firemen and Fort Monmouth neck-and-neck, requiring a three-game series to decide the Monmouth County Firemen's League Championship.

At the first game, September 23, 1934, at Fort Monmouth, Freehold overcame a seven-run deficit to tie the score 9–9. The game had to be stopped due to a heavy downpour of rain. Freehold lost the second game on the same day (at Manalapan field) by a score of 4–2, notwithstanding the noteworthy pitching of Lugannani, who fanned fourteen soldiers.

The final game, also at Manalapan field on September 30, 1934, was a nail-biter. Fort Monmouth got three runs in the fourth inning. In the seventh inning, Freehold matched their three runs. However, Fort Monmouth pushed across the winning run in the ninth inning, and Freehold couldn't duplicate the tally.[38]

The 1935 season brought a Firemen's League and Monmouth County Championship to the Freehold Firemen. Again, Quinn and Lugannani were the team's pitching powerhouses. Ira Matthews and Charley Haberman supported Quinn and Lugannani on the pitching mound.

My brother Dem was starting to play a lot of ball in the early to mid-1930s. (Please note that my father, David Demarest Cashion, and my brother, David Eugene Cashion, were both called Dem. My father was umpiring during the time my brother was playing.) My brother played for several clubs, including the Firemen. However, in 1935, he pitched against the Firemen twice.

The Firemen played the Freehold Holy Name team on September 7, 1935, at the Lincoln Place field to decide the Freehold championship. My brother pitched for the Holy Namers and Ira Matthews threw for the Firemen. Each man pitched a good game, fanning twelve men apiece. In a hard-fought game, the Holy Namers beat the Firemen 3–2.[39]

Also in 1935, the Monmouth County All-Stars, with Dem pitching, beat the Firemen 8–3 on November 3.[40] The leading batters in 1935 were Manuel at .438, I. Matthews at .417, Lugannani at .341, and Cashion at .333. Quinn led the pitching staff with a winning percentage of .583.[41] The winning team was presented with maroon jackets bearing a Maltese cross on the sleeve.

Some of the most interesting and successful money-raising events sponsored by the Firemen were donkey baseball games. The donkey game of 1935 had a reported attendance of 1,800 and brought in $175 to the fire department to benefit the baseball team.[42] Many Firemen ball players were seen riding toward first base astride donkeys. It was reported that other donkey baseball games were held in 1939, 1941, and 1942.

Another banner year for the Firemen was 1936. On July 31, Fred Quinn pitched a perfect game—no hits, no runs, no walks—and defeated Fort Monmouth 12-0.[43] Quinn had previously pitched a no-hitter shutout when he was a junior at Freehold High School. However, to this writer's knowledge, this is one of only two perfect games pitched in Freehold history. The second occurred eighteen years later by Ed Ostrowski.

Quinn continued his mastery over Fort Monmouth by pitching a 5–0 shutout against them on September 27, 1936, at the Fort Monmouth field. While Quinn threw a masterful game, he was aided by the terrific hitting of Billy Rhoades and Dem Cashion.[44] Quinn would throw right-handed in one game and left-handed in the next—truly an amazing pitcher.

The traditional annual supper of the Freehold Firemen Baseball Club was held at the Elks Club on February 3, 1937, with 114 members and guests enjoying a delicious meal. Appropriately, as the club's leading player, Quinn was the toastmaster.[45]

The Monmouth County Firemen's Baseball League collapsed in 1937. However, the Freehold Firemen's club continued to play independent ball for the next two years, with Oodles Vanderveer and "Scotty" Carswell appointed to arrange bookings.[46]

JUNIOR LEGION BASEBALL NINE

The 1933 Junior Legion was one of my brother Dave "Dem" Cashion's early baseball teams. From left to right on the front row: Jerry Sokol, Leo Dailey, Fred Rowe, Bennie Lazansky. Second row: Frank Witman, Arnold Tannenbaum, David Thompson, Lanier Shafto, John "Scotty" Carswell. Third row: Fred Runyon, Bill Thixton, Harold Waters, David Cashion. Courtesy of Cashion archives

Now is a good time to mention one of Freehold's most vital veteran's organizations, the American Legion Post 54. Founded on July 2, 1919, the Legion has been an integral part of Freehold for over one hundred years. On July 17, 1925, the National American Legion initiated a baseball league for young men. Post 54 of Freehold formed an American Legion team in 1928.

The team played until 1929, winning their fair share of games. Saker and Hyres formed the battery during those years.[47] The team was brought back to life in 1933–34 and

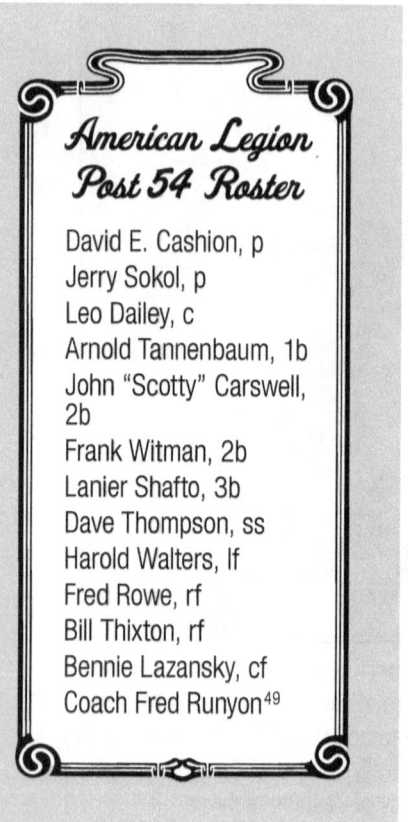

American Legion Post 54 Roster

David E. Cashion, p
Jerry Sokol, p
Leo Dailey, c
Arnold Tannenbaum, 1b
John "Scotty" Carswell, 2b
Frank Witman, 2b
Lanier Shafto, 3b
Dave Thompson, ss
Harold Walters, lf
Fred Rowe, rf
Bill Thixton, rf
Bennie Lazansky, cf
Coach Fred Runyon[49]

heralded the future Freehold star pitcher Dem Cashion. Wearing their newly acquired uniforms, the Freehold American Legion team fielded a stellar nine and drew a large number of spectators. They beat the Jamesburg Home for Boys 22–3 in June 1933 and advanced to the regionals.

Even at the young age of fourteen, my brother was already able to overpower batters. On June 24, 1933, he struck out fifteen Lakewood Legion players. On July 15, 1933, Cashion struck out fourteen Spotswood players. In June of 1934, he struck out seventeen while playing against the Hightstown Legion team.[48]

FHN Stands Out as Well

Another very successful Freehold baseball team was the aforementioned Freehold Holy Name (FHN). Percy Anderson was the brains behind this team when it was formed in 1935.

The FHN played exceptionally well in its first year, with Cashion quickly becoming the star pitcher and slugger. On August 16, 1935, the Holy Name club defeated the Footes A.C.s of Manalapan, who had come into the game with a string of fourteen consecutive wins, including defeating the Freehold Firemen championship team.[51]

FHN ended the 1935 season with a record of twenty-five wins and eleven losses, with five players batting over .300: Kuzava, .400; McGackin, .338; Quinn, .326; Cashion, .322; and McGlory, .300.[52]

The Holy Namers opened the 1936 season under new management. Gilday Freeman, former Villanova football star, served as manager and coach, with "Slats" Carey as assistant manager. By midyear, Freeman and Carey resigned, and Percy Anderson stepped back in as both manager and coach, with Ira Matthews serving as field captain.

The team's 1936 performance didn't match that of the previous year; however, they had some terrific wins behind the superb pitching of Cashion and the team's hitting, with nine FHN players batting over .300, including McGackin at .456 and Kuzava at .409. Three of the local players—Cashion, Narazonick, and McGackin—received a call to try out with the Newark Bears.[54]

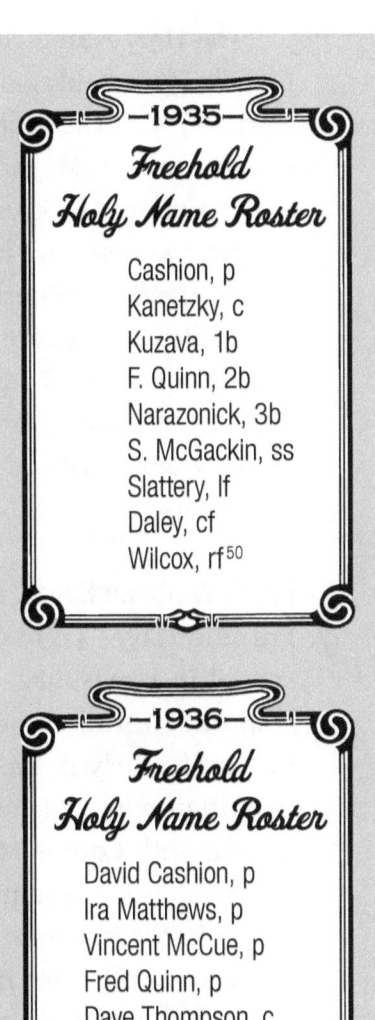

–1935–
*Freehold
Holy Name Roster*

Cashion, p
Kanetzky, c
Kuzava, 1b
F. Quinn, 2b
Narazonick, 3b
S. McGackin, ss
Slattery, lf
Daley, cf
Wilcox, rf[50]

–1936–
*Freehold
Holy Name Roster*

David Cashion, p
Ira Matthews, p
Vincent McCue, p
Fred Quinn, p
Dave Thompson, c
Stanley Narazonick, 2b
Ed Kuzava, 2b
Len McGackin, 3b
Joe McGlory, ss
John Arbaczawski, lf
Thomas Potter, cf
Fred Maher, rf
Ken Foster, rf[53]

The Holy Name club opened their 1937 season at the Lincoln Place field against the soldiers of Fort Monmouth on April 25, with the Fort Monmouth band providing rousing entertainment. Mayor Peter F. Runyon tossed out the first ball to County Clerk Joseph McDermott. The batters who hit the first and second home runs would be awarded grand prizes of a five-dollar hat and a stem of bananas.

Oodles Vanderveer had joined the club, and he hit a single to help FHN squeeze out a 3–2 victory on June 26, 1937, over Demura Athletic Association (A.A.) of Nutley. Dave "Dem" Cashion helped the cause with his fifteen strikeouts.[55]

Frank Whitman Hayes: A Six-Time All-Star

Frankie Hayes (1914–1955) attended grammar and high school in Jamesburg, New Jersey. He received a scholarship to Pennington Seminary based on his athletic ability, particularly in baseball. After Hayes graduated from Pennington in 1934, he went to Shibe Park, Philadelphia, to try out with Connie Mack's Philadelphia Athletics. He impressed Mack and joined the team, becoming the youngest player in the major leagues.

However, before he joined the major leagues, Hayes roamed the outfield and played catcher for the Freehold Pirates and the Vanderveer Freehold ball clubs in 1932 and 1933, proving his baseball prowess by hitting several home runs. His family moved to 92 East Main Street, Freehold, circa 1935, and his brother attended Freehold High School. Hayes spent some time in the minors in 1935 and squeezed in a game catching for Freehold Holy Name on October 19, 1935. My brother was his battery mate for that game.[56]

Hayes was a six-time All-Star and holds the major league record for consecutive games by a catcher (312). He played for the Athletics for nine years and the St. Louis Browns for two years, then went back to Philadelphia for one year, to Cleveland for a year, and to the Chicago White Sox and the Boston Red Sox for another year.

Hayes was the Indians' catcher on April 30, 1946, when Bob Feller threw a no-hitter, and he provided the only run of the game with a ninth-inning home run. At the end of his career, Hayes returned to New Jersey and opened a sporting goods store in Point Pleasant. He died at the young age of forty.

Early in Hayes's major league career, he participated in a once-in-a-lifetime experience. In October 1934, Mack took a star-studded All-Star baseball team to Japan for a series of exhibition games. Mack's squad included Lou Gehrig, Jimmie Foxx, Lefty Gomez, and Babe Ruth. The two catchers assigned to the All-Star team were Charlie Berry from the Athletics and Moe Berg from Cleveland.

At the last minute, Berry could not make the trip, and Mack called on Hayes to join the team. The Japanese reception for the "Babe" was exceptional, with over 100,000 lining the Ginza to see Ruth and shout "Banzi Bambino!" "Bonzai Babe!" The series saw the American baseball heroes delight the crowd. Babe hit two homers in the farewell game, and Foxx and Gehrig contributed home runs as they beat the Nippon All-Stars 15–6. The whole American lineup shifted each inning, with Ruth and five others playing seven positions.[57]

While the catching duties for the American All-Stars were to have alternated between Berg and Hayes, that arrangement didn't materialize. Berg caught the first game and a few more, but most of the games were caught by Hayes.

Frankie Hayes, all-star catcher and member of Connie Mack's 1934 Japan tour.
Photo by George Rinhart/Corbis Historical via Getty Images

On November 29, the American team pounded the
Japanese team 23–5. Hayes was the catcher, and Berg was
not at the game. He had allegedly left to visit a friend at

St. Luke's Hospital. The hospital was a seven-story structure, unusually tall for Tokyo. When he arrived, Berg donned a kimono and proceeded to the roof, where there was a panoramic view of Tokyo.

From beneath his kimono, Berg took out a movie camera. For four hours, he nervously recorded the surrounding city, including shipyards, industrial complexes, and military installations around Tokyo. After his filming, he hid the camera beneath his kimono and inconspicuously left the hospital, without visiting anyone there .[58]

Approximately seven and a half years later, Berg turned the films over to the FBI and military intelligence. They were among the photographs used in the April 18, 1942, Jimmy Doolittle attack on the Japanese mainland. Berg, a native of Newark, a Princeton and Columbia law school alum, and a linguist with fluency in approximately seventeen languages, was an early associ-

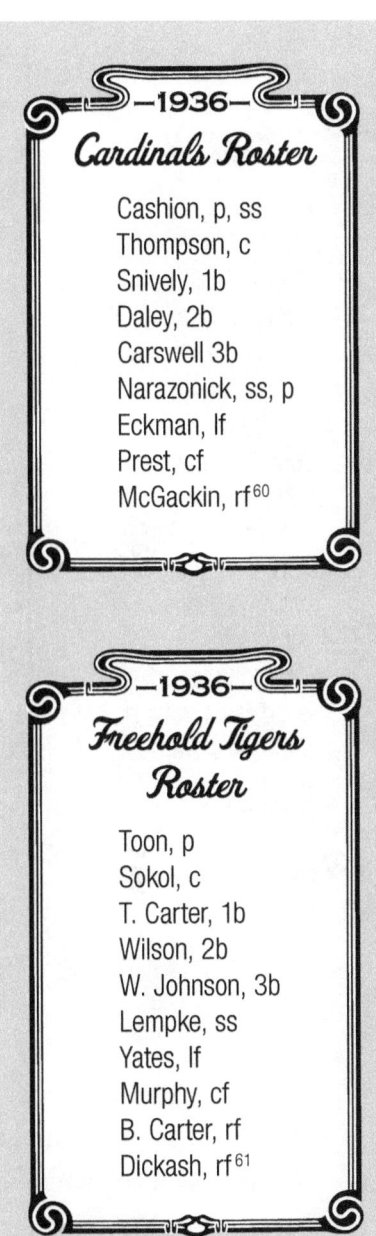

–1936–
Cardinals Roster

Cashion, p, ss
Thompson, c
Snively, 1b
Daley, 2b
Carswell 3b
Narazonick, ss, p
Eckman, lf
Prest, cf
McGackin, rf[60]

–1936–
Freehold Tigers Roster

Toon, p
Sokol, c
T. Carter, 1b
Wilson, 2b
W. Johnson, 3b
Lempke, ss
Yates, lf
Murphy, cf
B. Carter, rf
Dickash, rf[61]

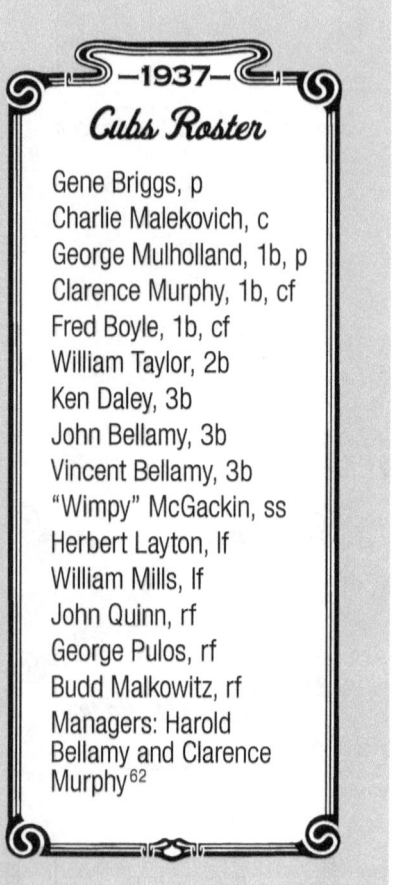

—1937—

Cubs Roster

Gene Briggs, p
Charlie Malekovich, c
George Mulholland, 1b, p
Clarence Murphy, 1b, cf
Fred Boyle, 1b, cf
William Taylor, 2b
Ken Daley, 3b
John Bellamy, 3b
Vincent Bellamy, 3b
"Wimpy" McGackin, ss
Herbert Layton, lf
William Mills, lf
John Quinn, rf
George Pulos, rf
Budd Malkowitz, rf
Managers: Harold
Bellamy and Clarence
Murphy[62]

ate of the Office of Strategic Services (OSS), the precursor to the CIA, and served the United States intelligence services for many years.[59]

Two other Freehold ball clubs had short-lived operations in 1936. As was common practice, the players on these two teams played on other local teams. Freehold baseball players must have had several different baseball uniforms in their closets.

A different team that was formed in 1937 had more longevity than the two mentioned above. The Freehold Cubs baseball squad started in early 1937 and lasted through 1940. The team consisted of players from high school, the local rug mill, and elsewhere. It was a team designed to give the players experience so they could advance to other teams in Freehold. By July, it was boasting eleven wins and one loss. In August of 1937, the Cubs took on 40 A.C., the local Black team, which had been very active in the late 1920s.

The caliber of baseball in Freehold improved throughout the first three decades of the twentieth century. Several trophies were awarded to Freehold's championship teams and foreshadowed even more diamond action on Freehold's baseball fields.

In the decades coming, we'll learn about the father of Freehold baseball, witness an incredible number of no-hitters, and relive this author's glory days.

1937-1973: FIERCE COMPETITION

*"There are three things you can do in a baseball game.
You can win, or you can lose, or it will rain."*
—CASEY STENGEL

reehold baseball continued its explosion in the late 1930s. The reasons for this growth were varied. Some of it had to do with the success of many of the local teams from the 1900s through the mid-1930s. Other factors included the increase in population and the improving economic growth in Freehold.

In any case, the number of baseball clubs hit an all-time high, and games were played at the Manalapan Avenue and Lincoln Place fields several times a week. Until World War II took so many men away from the local diamonds, baseball was the entertainment king of Freehold. Following World War II, there were fewer clubs; however, high-caliber baseball teams continued to play from the mid-1940s through the early 1970s.

In early 1938, the Freehold Holy Name team was starting to organize for the new season. However, a new team came on the scene, and the Holy Namers were absorbed into that team. The new team, the Gulistans, sponsored by A. & M. Karagheusian (the rug mill), was formed in March, initially piloted by Percy Anderson.

In mid-season, Dick Skehan took over the reins of the team. Many of the players were familiar to residents.

Behind the strong arms of the Gulistans' pitchers, the team did very well in its first year. They won the Northern Division of the Monmouth County Semi-Pro League. However, they were defeated in the state tournament with a pitiful 7-0 loss to Glen Gardner at Dunn Field in Trenton.[2]

The 1938 season was a busy year for baseball players, with new teams popping up and players bouncing from team to team. The "Texas" Indians lasted from 1938 to mid-1939. The area of Freehold where the rug mill was located was named "Texas," with the derivation of the name lost in antiquity. It is believed that the Indians were a team made up of rug mill players who didn't play on the Gulistan team. They managed to win a few games during their tenure, but they were on the losing column in most games.

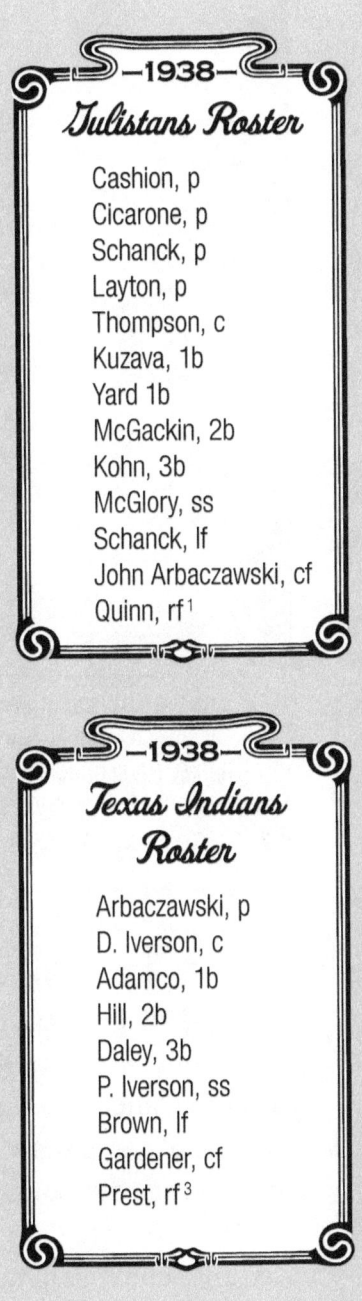

–1938–

Gulistans Roster

Cashion, p
Cicarone, p
Schanck, p
Layton, p
Thompson, c
Kuzava, 1b
Yard 1b
McGackin, 2b
Kohn, 3b
McGlory, ss
Schanck, lf
John Arbaczawski, cf
Quinn, rf[1]

–1938–

Texas Indians Roster

Arbaczawski, p
D. Iverson, c
Adamco, 1b
Hill, 2b
Daley, 3b
P. Iverson, ss
Brown, lf
Gardener, cf
Prest, rf[3]

1938 was the first year of the Gulistan team. From left to right on the front row: Frank Quinn, Joe McGlory, Thomas Layton, Ed Kuzava, Melchoir Sniveley. Second row: Stanley Narsen, John Arbaczwaski, David Cashion, David Thompson, Len McGackin. Third row: Henry Schanck, Pat Cicarone, Barney Kohn, Joe Arbaczwaski, Roger Yard, Benjamin Benton. Courtesy of Roberta Schanck collection

The Indians team was removed from the county league in June 1939 on three counts: failure to appear for a scheduled game with the Manasquan A.C.s, failure to pay the entry fee, and no compliance with the league ruling about filing a player's list.[4] The team did resurface in 1941, although they did not have a full season schedule.

The Freehold Cubs had a good start in 1937, and it carried into their 1938 to 1940 seasons. Powered by the slugging of Dante Federici, who joined the club in 1938, the

Cubs had very successful seasons during their days on the Firemen's Field.

One of the Cubs' frequent opponents in the 1938 and 1939 seasons was the Freehold Grays, a young local Black team. The Grays came out on the losing side but played gallantly. The May 14, 1939, encounter was an absolute slugfest, with the Cubs winning 21–15.

Two other Black teams of the late 1930s and early 1940s were the Dunbars and the Freehold Eagles. During this time period, a leading sponsor of Black baseball was the Red Ball Inn, located on the Freehold-Hightstown road.

One of the most successful ball clubs from 1938 to 1943 was the Cosmopolitan Baseball Club (Cosmos). This club was organized at a meeting at Goldstein's store on Center Avenue in Freehold (in the area known as "Texas") in March 1938. The team joined the Monmouth County Sunday Baseball Circuit. Officers of the club were President John Lang,

–1939–

Texas Indians Roster

Higgins, p
Taylor, c
Alexander, 1b
E. Lempke, 2b
Tela, 3b
Accisano, ss
Iverson, lf
Lafayette, cf
Belaski, rf[5]

–1938–

Freehold Grays Roster

Pierce, p
Morris, p
Conover, c
Matthews, c
Person, 1b
Ballentine, 2b
Sparks, 3b
Lewis, 3b
Edgerton, ss
Robinson, ss
Brodie, lf
Ruth, c
Stiles, cf[6]

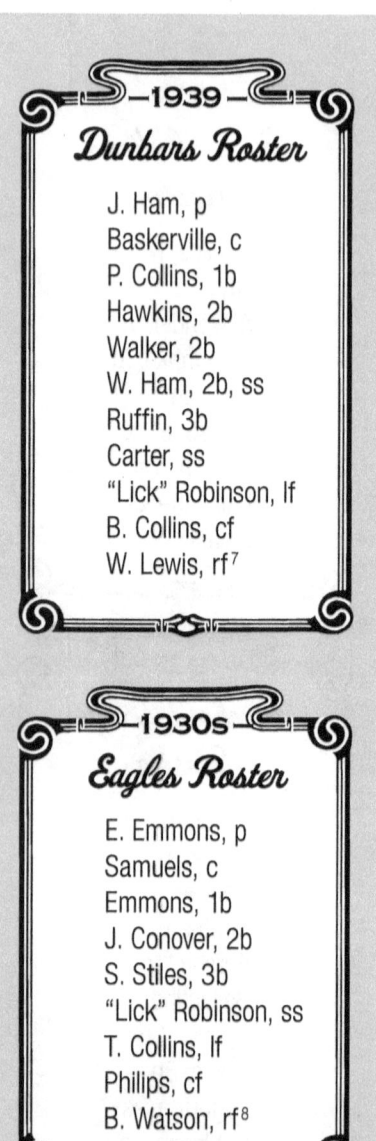

-1939-

Dunbars Roster

J. Ham, p
Baskerville, c
P. Collins, 1b
Hawkins, 2b
Walker, 2b
W. Ham, 2b, ss
Ruffin, 3b
Carter, ss
"Lick" Robinson, lf
B. Collins, cf
W. Lewis, rf[7]

-1930s-

Eagles Roster

E. Emmons, p
Samuels, c
Emmons, 1b
J. Conover, 2b
S. Stiles, 3b
"Lick" Robinson, ss
T. Collins, lf
Philips, cf
B. Watson, rf[8]

Treasurer Gilbert Toon, and Secretary and Manager Curtis Yates.[9]

Playing on the Freehold High School field, the Cosmos were a solid team. They were initially coached by Leon Weinstein, with David Reichey taking over the reins in 1941.

"Gibby" Toon, ace pitcher, lost a tough game to the West Belmar team on May 1, 1938. After mowing down twenty opposition batters, the Cosmos finally lost 3–1.[11] Gibby would continue his sensational hurling for the Cosmos and other teams for several years.

The Father of Freehold Baseball: David Eugene "Dem" Cashion

As mentioned previously, E. I. Vanderveer was called the Grandfather of Freehold Baseball, and I would like to add here that my brother, "Dem" Cashion, was clearly the Father of Freehold Baseball.

Cashion entered the Freehold baseball arena in 1933 and departed from baseball shortly before his death in April 1976. His playing days, primarily as a pitcher, and at first base when not on the mound, began with American Legion baseball and ended with the 1973 Freehold team. He managed many local teams and umpired for many years, and in the early 1970s was making a case for the creation of a Jersey Shore Baseball Hall of Fame.

Cashion's fastball, curveball, and tantalizing knuckleball led him to be the dominant pitcher in Monmouth County from the mid-1930s to the mid-1950s. While his fastball slowed a bit, he continued to be able to get batters out well into the mid-1960s. And he never lost his batting eye.

Cashion lived and breathed baseball, following his father's path. Local ball clubs constantly sought him to play for them,

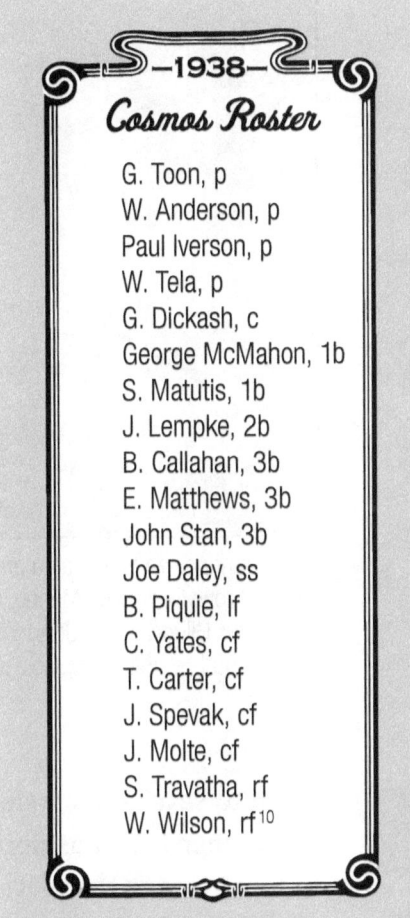

—1938—

Cosmos Roster

G. Toon, p
W. Anderson, p
Paul Iverson, p
W. Tela, p
G. Dickash, c
George McMahon, 1b
S. Matutis, 1b
J. Lempke, 2b
B. Callahan, 3b
E. Matthews, 3b
John Stan, 3b
Joe Daley, ss
B. Piquie, lf
C. Yates, cf
T. Carter, cf
J. Spevak, cf
J. Molte, cf
S. Travatha, rf
W. Wilson, rf[10]

which he did. On June 8, 1938, while playing for the Freehold Firemen, Cashion pitched a no-hitter, striking out eleven.[12] The umpire for this game was the elder Dem Cashion, who, surely, called a fair game.

The younger Cashion played for the Englishtown Sporting Club team and used his batting prowess to carry

The Cosmopolitan team had a great run from 1938 to 1943. From left to right on the front row: George McMahon, George Dickash, Bill Tela, Joe Daley, Bill Wilson. Back row: Gilbert Toon, John Stan, Coach Leon Weinstein, Curtis Yates, Paul Iverson. Batboy: Bill Daley. Courtesy of Monmouth County Historical Association

them to several victories. Against the Manasquan A.C.s in September 1938, Cashion pounded out three extra-base hits in four trips to the plate.[13]

During his local playing career, Cashion played for the Freehold American Legion, Freehold Cardinals, Freehold Firemen, Sayreville National Lead, Englishtown Sporting Club, Freehold Holy Name, Belmar All-Stars, Red Bank Pirates, Belmar Braves, Brooklyn Bushwicks, Freehold Merchants, Freehold Gulistans, Freehold Townsmen, and Freehold County Seaters.

Cashion was under contract with the Washington Senators in 1940 and played with their Salisbury, Maryland, minor league team in the Eastern Shore League. In 1948 and

1949, Cashion played with the Washington Senators' minor league team in Kingston, New York, in the Colonial League.

We will learn more about the younger Dem Cashion in the chapters subtitled "One of Freehold's Best" and "He Lived it Until the End."

Another Freehold baseball club revived in 1940 was the Holy Name Baseball Club, under its former manager Percy Anderson. "All youths from 17 to 24 years of age who were interested were asked to attend the organization meet-

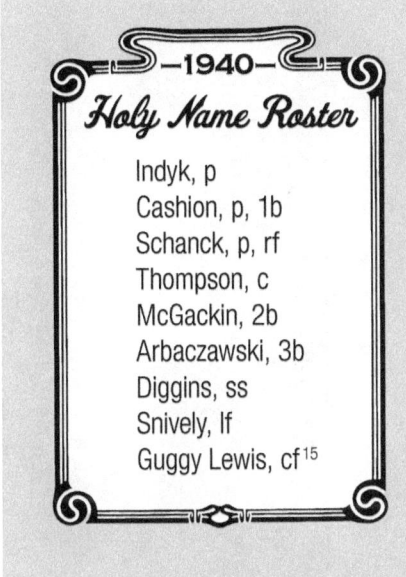

—1940—
Holy Name Roster

Indyk, p
Cashion, p, 1b
Schanck, p, rf
Thompson, c
McGackin, 2b
Arbaczawski, 3b
Diggins, ss
Snively, lf
Guggy Lewis, cf[15]

ing at the Knights of Columbus Home."[14] The assembled team comprised names familiar to local baseball fans.

The Holy Name team now had two Black ball players with Hank Schanck and the addition of "Guggy" Lewis. The 1941 Holy Name team added a few top-notch players: Joe McGlory, shortstop, Dante Federici, first baseman, Harry Burt, pitcher, and Layton, outfield. M. Tyrell was the president of the club, Percy Anderson remained as manager, and Dave Thompson was the assistant manager and captain.[16]

The Holy Name club ended its baseball days by winning the 1941 Shore Sunday Baseball League Championship. In the third game of a three-game playoff, Paul Dolan of the Holy Name club allowed only five scattered hits, and Holy Name beat Point Pleasant 6–2. Cashion led the sluggers in this contest by going three for four, including a double.[17]

The 1938 Freehold Firemen team included Alvah "Oodles" Vanderveer (top row, second from left) and E. I. Vanderveer (third from left). Courtesy of Nolan Higgins

On May 30, 1940, Holy Name battled the House of David. The famous House of David team played several Freehold teams during the late 1930s and mid-1940s. On June 9, 1938, the Freehold Firemen beat the bearded House of David team 17–3.

The House of David always brought floodlights, so their games were held at night, with large crowds in attendance. The Firemen sluggers for the June 9 game were Dane, with four hits, and Manuel, Egbert, and Allen, with three hits apiece. The elder Cashion was the umpire for that game.[18]

On May 12, 1939, the Freehold Gulistans beat the House of David 5–3. Cashion pitched the entire game, striking out thirteen batters and allowing eight scattered hits. Manager

Roger Yard had two hits, including a home run, to lead the Gulistans' offensive attack.[19]

House of David: Bearded and Badass

The bearded House of David team, with their baseball antics, always attracted a large crowd. Their diamond performance was also of high caliber. One of the pitchers on the House of David team in the early 1940s was a Freehold native, Michael Janesko. My brother said that Jimmy Woods, a House of David player, was the best first baseman he had ever seen. Cashion said, "Woods couldn't hit the side of a barn, but he was to first base what Goose Tatum was to basketball."[20]

"The House of David is a religious order founded in 1903 in Benton Harbor, Michigan. They were strong contributors to the agricultural community around them . . . they developed one of the first cold storage facilities in the country . . . they developed a pre-Disney type amusement park, complete with miniature trains. They were credited with inventing the automatic pinsetter used in bowling alleys. . . .

"Another tenet of their faith was that they must neither shave nor cut their hair. Consequently, team members wore long hair and beards as they played.

"The team's players were motivated by the need to make money for their families and colony back home.

"The feature for which the House of David is perhaps best remembered, however, is the talented teams of bearded barnstorming baseball players that traveled to nearly every state in the Union, Mexico, and most of the Canadian provinces from the 1920s to the 1950s.

"Grover Cleveland Alexander would serve as manager/ pitcher for one of the House of David teams from 1931 to 1935. In 1934, Babe Didrikson Zaharias joined the Eastern

The House of David from the 1940s was a very exciting, entertaining, and talented team. Courtesy of Dorn's Classic Images

traveling team, adding, uniquely, a female to the team. That same year, Satchel Paige signed to play with the House of David, twelve years before Jackie Robinson integrated organized baseball with Montreal, playing his first game at Jersey City in 1946."[21]

"The House of David is credited with inventing the 'Pepper Game,' which was along the lines of the fancy basketball moves of the Harlem Globetrotters."[22] This pregame warm-up drill was a delight for the Freehold fans, and it became a standard drill for all local ball clubs. I vividly remember introducing the pepper game to my teammates at Brown University in the early 1960s.

Essentially, one player would act as the batter and stand twenty feet from four or so teammates. He would hit a one-hopper to the first teammate, and the teammate would send it back to him, and so on. Sometimes the players would horse around by tossing the ball among themselves during this drill.

Charlie "Malko" Malekovich was another member of Freehold's baseball elite. Malekovich was a good ball player from high school through the 1940s. He became manager of a couple of local Freehold teams, was instrumental in forming the Babe Ruth League, and coached in that league for decades.

He was my coach on the Red Sox team of the Babe Ruth League in the early 1950s. Malko was an umpire for the Southern New Jersey Umpire Association for more than

> **—1942—**
> ## Trylons Roster
> Bob Throckmorton, p
> Ira Matthews, p
> Brown, p
> Demko, p, ss
> Mickey Quinn, c
> Dante Federici, 1b
> Madge, 2b
> Malekovich, 2b
> Filan, 3b
> "Pinky" Higgins, ss
> Joe Parenteau, lf
> Tom Brereton, cf
> Burt, rf
> Gene Briggs, rf [23]

forty years. He managed the Trylon ball club from 1939 to 1942. The Trylons were mainly local players who had graduated from Freehold High School within the past four years.

My brother continued to lead the Freehold Gulistans from 1939 until mid-1940. The Gulistans, managed by Roger Yard in May 1939, defeated the Riverside Field club at Firemen's Field in Freehold, with Dem pitching a two-hit shutout, 2–0. [24]

In mid-1940, Cashion joined the Salisbury, Maryland, minor league team. On October 6, 1940, he was honored at a Freehold All-Star game, with the Holy Namers pitted

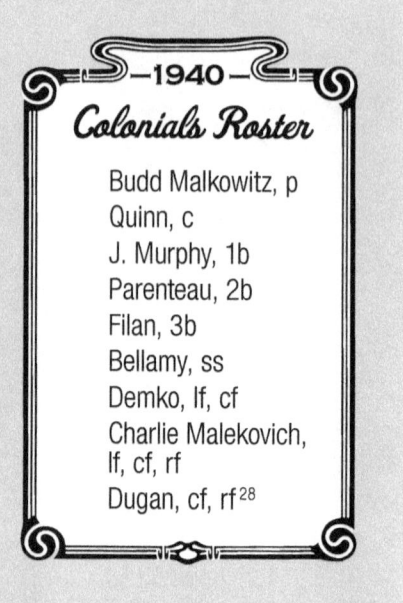

—1940—
Colonials Roster

Budd Malkowitz, p
Quinn, c
J. Murphy, 1b
Parenteau, 2b
Filan, 3b
Bellamy, ss
Demko, lf, cf
Charlie Malekovich,
lf, cf, rf
Dugan, cf, rf[28]

against the Freehold All-Stars. Cashion demonstrated why he was playing professionally by pitching a three-hitter for the winning Holy Name club.[25]

In May of 1941, Cashion also joined Toon and Lennie McGackin from Freehold on the Monmouth County All-Star team in a contest against the Belmar Braves.[26] And, in June 1941, Cashion donned the uniform of the Belmar Braves. He was scheduled to pitch against the Brooklyn Royal Giants; however, the game was rained out. He did pitch and garner the win against the Detroit Clowns, 9–5.[27]

Another team that lasted for the 1940 and 1941 seasons was the Freehold Colonials. Many of the players on the Colonials team also played on the Trylons club.

Many baseball teams dwindled as the Freehold players slowly left the town from 1942 to 1945 to join their military brethren in Asia and Europe. However, enough players remained in town to field a few teams. For example, the Freehold A.C.s played from 1942 through 1944. Before Cashion left for military service, he pitched for this team in 1942.

During their three-year run, the Freehold A.C.s, under the leadership of Percy Anderson, relied on the pitching staff of Tela, Hendrickson, and Palladino, a star of the Englishtown Sporting Club. The other players on the Freehold A.C. team were Kuzava, Diggins, Layton, Farmer, O'Neill, Ruggiero, Serratelli, Narazonick, B. Salkowitz, T. Salkowitz, Prest, and Madge.[29]

Also during this period, there were two active Black baseball clubs. The Freehold Colored Giants played against a team of Black soldiers from Camp Dix at the Manalapan grounds on Decoration Day in 1942.

The second team, the Freehold Brown Bombers, played in 1944. On July 4, 1944, they defeated "the Lakewood colored team on the Manalapan Avenue diamond by 6–2. This was the 'rubber.' The Lakewood

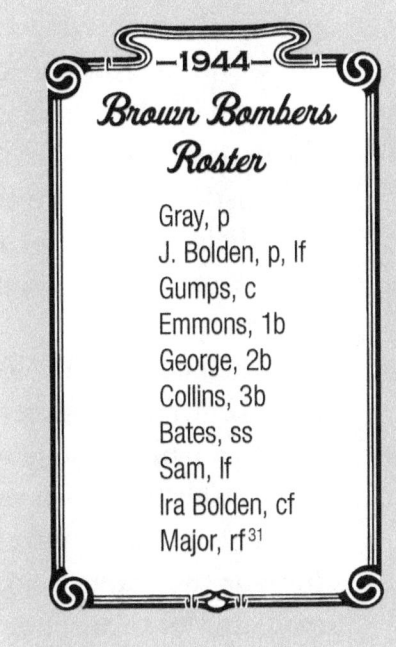

–1944–
Brown Bombers Roster

Gray, p
J. Bolden, p, lf
Gumps, c
Emmons, 1b
George, 2b
Collins, 3b
Bates, ss
Sam, lf
Ira Bolden, cf
Major, rf[31]

team had defeated the locals in a game at Lakewood a few weeks ago by the score of 5–4, which had to go 11 innings for the decision. The Brown Bombers defeated the same team the previous week by 8–7."[30]

In a hotly contested game on August 27, 1944, the Brown Bombers defeated the Freehold A.C. club 5–3, behind the solid Brown Bomber pitching of Gray and J. Bolden.

Before TV and Cell Phones, Baseball was King

I can vividly recall my earliest memories of watching grown men play baseball on the Institute Place field in the 1940s. Long before social media, cell phones, and the advent of television, families would enjoy Sunday afternoons at the ballpark. I would walk one block, meander through a dirt path to the field, and join the throng.

A typical crowd of 500–700 would enjoy watching their husbands, fathers, uncles, brothers, and friends take part in the national pastime. Within the boundaries of Hull Avenue and Institute Place, stretching out toward Ramcat Alley in right field and the Freehold Military School in deep center field, hundreds of ball players played ball for decades on that diamond.

When not in the field, the players sat on benches, single pieces of timber approximately thirty feet long. There was always a pail of water, with a ladle for the players to gulp some water to quench their thirst.

Spectators who got to the park early were lucky enough to sit on the grandstand, about five rows high, situated immediately in back of home plate. The remaining spectators brought chairs and blankets and positioned themselves down the first and third base sidelines. Refreshments of soda and water were sold from large ice buckets on the sidelines.

As foul balls shot over the grandstand and rolled down the hill on Hull Avenue, local boys would scurry to retrieve the balls in hopes of earning a dime or a quarter. At midpoint in the game, someone would take a hat from a local player and pass it among the spectators. On a good day, twenty dollars would be collected from the crowd.

The crowds were always enthusiastic, and the players always did their best to provide a hard-fought contest.

Go Gulistans!

The ball players who had returned from the fighting in Asia and Europe were anxious to get back on the baseball diamond. In April 1946, Gene Briggs became coach and Norman

Miles manager of the reconstituted Freehold Gulistan Athletic Association (A.A.) ball club. The team would join the recently formed Jersey Shore Baseball League.

Many former members of the Freehold Trylons, Cosmos, and early Gulistans joined in hopes of producing a formidable nine, and they accomplished that goal. The strongest element of the new Gulistans was the team's mound strength: Dem Cashion, already an acknowledged star pitcher, Bill Tela, a member of the earlier Gulistan A.A. team, "Gibby" Toon, a former Cosmos star, and Harry Burt.

Dave Thompson, Cashion's old battery mate, was the catcher. Dante Federici, a former Trylon star, held down first base; Briggs, Sam McGackin, and Ken Daley worked the keystone combination. Dayton Wilson was at third. In the outfield were Tom Brereton, Herb Layton, and Ed Jerolis. Utility men were Ed Lempke and Hank Schanck. Schanck also assisted Briggs as coach.[32]

The 1946 Gulistans had an excellent season. By mid-August, they were 11–2 and in first place, one game ahead of the tough Red Bank Towners. On August 11, 1946, the Gulistans defeated Keyport 7–1. Cashion was the winning pitcher and set a Jersey Shore League record by striking out seventeen men. Cashion and Arbaczawski led the offensive charge with two hits apiece.[33] The Gulistans narrowly lost the '46 Jersey Shore Championship to the Red Bank Towners, but they would avenge that loss in the future.

A photo of the 1946 Gulistan team shows the players wearing various uniforms, some with Gulistan shirts, some with Holy Name shirts. The team was "founded on $100. And that money was gone the first few weeks of the campaign. The only way that Gene Briggs has been able to get by on such a paltry sum was by reneging on uniforms for the play-

FREEHOLD BASEBALL TEAM TAKES A BOW

The 1946 Gulistans marked the start of a powerhouse team. From left to right on the front row: Ed Lempke, Herbert Layton, Joe McGlory, Bill Tela, "Gugie" Lewis, E. Briggs, Tom Brereton. Back row: Len McGackin, Marty Diggins, Dave Thompson, Dave Cashion, Ed Jerolis, Dayton Wilson. Batboy: Wally Cook. Courtesy of Monmouth County Historical Association

ers. The men were to bring anything they could get a hold of. The only thing the club agreed to provide were stockings. And that is the reason 'our champions' look so ragged."[34]

The 1947 Gulistan team competed with another Freehold team in the Jersey Shore League. Charlie "Malko" Malekovich reinvigorated the Freehold A.C. club and produced stiff competition for the Gulistans. The Freehold A.C. club and the Gulistans played top-notch ball for the next few seasons.

The 1947 Gulistan team kept winning games with outstanding pitching and prodigious slugging. Cashion set down sixteen on strikes in a rare night game against the Red Bank Towners on the Shrewsbury Avenue field in Red

Bank on July 31, 1947.[35] On July 27, 1947, the Gulistans offered no mercy to St. Mary's of Port Monmouth, with a 19–0 win. The win was marked by the sensational hitting of Carl "Swede" Hansen, who smacked two homers, two triples, and a double for a perfect day at the plate. Sam McGackin contributed to the hitting onslaught with two triples, a double, and a single.[36]

In another game, Cashion led the team to a win with two home runs in a 3–2 victory against the Red Bank Braves on August 24, 1947.[37] They were heading for the championship round between their team and either Asbury Park or Freehold A.C.

Charlie Malko's Freehold A.C. club vied for the right to go against the Gulistans by playing Asbury Park in August 1947. Going into the ninth inning, the score was 12–6 in favor of Asbury Park. The Freehold A.C. club fought hard and came within a run of winning the game.

The Gulistans had swept the two-game series from the Keyport American Legion with a 5–3 victory to annex the National Division of the Jersey Shore League. In this game, Swede Hansen, a mighty slugger, drove in all five runs with a home run and a single.[38]

Thus, the Gulistans went against Asbury Park, the winner of the American Division, for the Jersey Shore Championship. The best-of-three series started at the Lincoln Place field before about a thousand spectators. The Gulistans beat the Asbury Park nine 4–3, with the winning run knocked in by Dante Federici. In the second game, the Gulistans had little problem defeating Asbury Park by a score of 6–2, becoming the 1947 Jersey Shore League champions.[39]

The Gulistan champions entered the 1948 season with the same strong team and performed in a stellar manner.

Jersey of Freehold Gulistan team. Courtesy of Monmouth County Historical Association

The team played well throughout the season and then, in September, Cashion returned from his minor league stint with Kingston, New York, and, coupled with Ralph Steinberg's strong arm, the team's performance ratcheted up a notch.

In September, "the Gulistans combined a 20-hit barrage with the spectacular two-hit pitching of 'Dem.' Indyk sparked the hitting spree with four hits, but 'Dem' aided his cause with a double and a home run."[40] Later that month,

Cashion hurled two shutouts: Long Branch 17–0 and West Belmar Blackhawks 4–0.[41] The Gulistans found themselves back in the playoffs for the 1948 Jersey Shore Championship.

The first game in the three-game series was won by the Gulistans 3–2 on Newman Springs field in Red Bank. The second game was a real nail-biter at the Lincoln Place field in Freehold. The almost one thousand fans at the game saw the Gulistans jump to a lead, only to have the Red Bank Towners come back in the fifth inning with a two-run home run to give the Red Bank Towners the winning margin of 8–7. Guggy Lewis's triple and Dante Federici's towering home run provided the slugging for the Gulistans, but it was not enough.

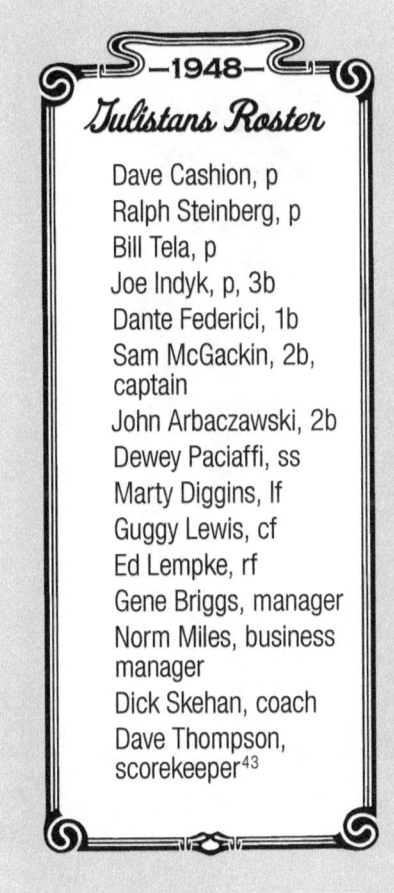

—1948—
Gulistans Roster

Dave Cashion, p
Ralph Steinberg, p
Bill Tela, p
Joe Indyk, p, 3b
Dante Federici, 1b
Sam McGackin, 2b, captain
John Arbaczawski, 2b
Dewey Paciaffi, ss
Marty Diggins, lf
Guggy Lewis, cf
Ed Lempke, rf
Gene Briggs, manager
Norm Miles, business manager
Dick Skehan, coach
Dave Thompson, scorekeeper[43]

On a coin toss, Lincoln Place was designated as the venue for the third decisive game. Before another massive crowd of approximately one thousand, Cashion was on the mound and came through with flying colors. His six-hit pitching, combined with a solid ten-hit attack, carried the day for the Gulistans. They easily won the game 8–2 and repeated as Jersey Shore champions.[42]

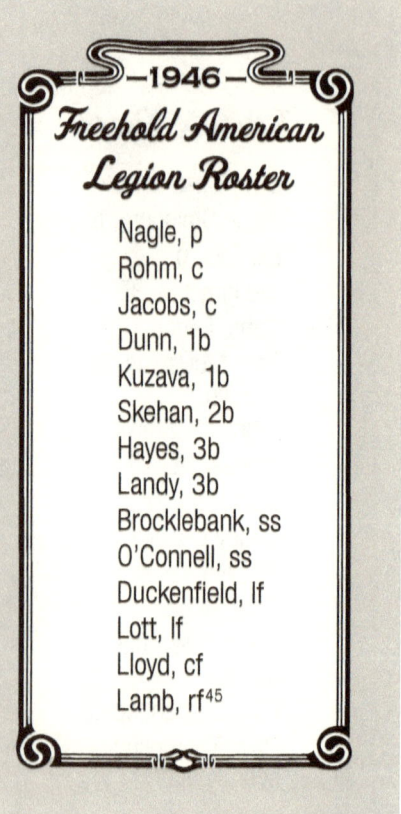

— 1946 —

Freehold American Legion Roster

Nagle, p
Rohm, c
Jacobs, c
Dunn, 1b
Kuzava, 1b
Skehan, 2b
Hayes, 3b
Landy, 3b
Brocklebank, ss
O'Connell, ss
Duckenfield, lf
Lott, lf
Lloyd, cf
Lamb, rf[45]

Bill Tela became the manager of the Gulistans in 1949. The following two seasons did not match the records of 1947 and 1948.

The Freehold American Legion had a couple of "rebirths" during the postwar era. In 1946, they sponsored a Junior American Legion team for four seasons. They played decent ball during this period. On June 20, 1947, Mickey Nagle came within one pitch of hurling a perfect game and defeated Spring Lake by the score of 7–0.[44] John Palmeri served as manager during the four seasons.

Lester "Lick" Robinson was a Black ball player who played alongside Schanck in the late 1930s into the mid-1940s. Lick was a member of several local teams, including the Freehold Eagles, Freehold Holy Name, the Freehold Brown Bombers, the National Lead, and the Gulistans.

Robinson moved to Columbus, Ohio, in 1947. In 1948, he was one of the Ohio State News Baseball Talent Pool candidates. The outcome of the pool would give the first three winners a chance to go to the St. Louis Cardinal-sponsored baseball tryout camp at Red Bird Stadium in June.[46] Unfortunately, there was no recorded result of the poll's outcome.

Ralph Steinberg: King of the Rubber

Ralph Steinberg was active on the Freehold diamonds for only four years; however, his pitching prowess during those four years was unmatched in Freehold's baseball history. While at Freehold High School in 1948, Steinberg's pitching earned him All-Shore and All-State honors. In 1947, Mayor Fred Quinn was instrumental in getting Steinberg, along with Werner "Joe" Rohm and George Lloyd, a tryout with the St. Louis Cardinals in Asbury Park. Unfortunately, none of the men made the team, although Steinberg and Rohm had subsequent tryouts with other major league teams.

On April 27, 1948, while in high school, Steinberg pitched a no-hit, no-run game against Toms River, with a score of 2–0, while striking out thirteen.[47] The following week, on May 6, 1948, Steinberg hurled another no-hit game against Toms River, 6–1.[48] He was on fire, and on May 24, 1948, with scouts from the Detroit Tigers and the Philadelphia Phillies looking on, he missed another no-hitter by a leadoff single. He won the game easily 9–1 and set a Shore Conference record with sixteen strikeouts.[49]

In June, Steinberg, along with Rohm and Bobby Hayes, worked out at Ebbets Field. Hayes was Steinberg's battery mate at Freehold High School. Hayes was the younger brother of Frankie Hayes, and he had tremendous baseball success in his high school days.

Steinberg decided to attend Tampa University and delay any minor league aspirations. He pitched well there. The one year that Tampa did not field a team, Steinberg pitched semipro ball for the Cuban Centro Asturiano team. He set a strikeout record for the Florida league, retiring eighteen batters in a single game.

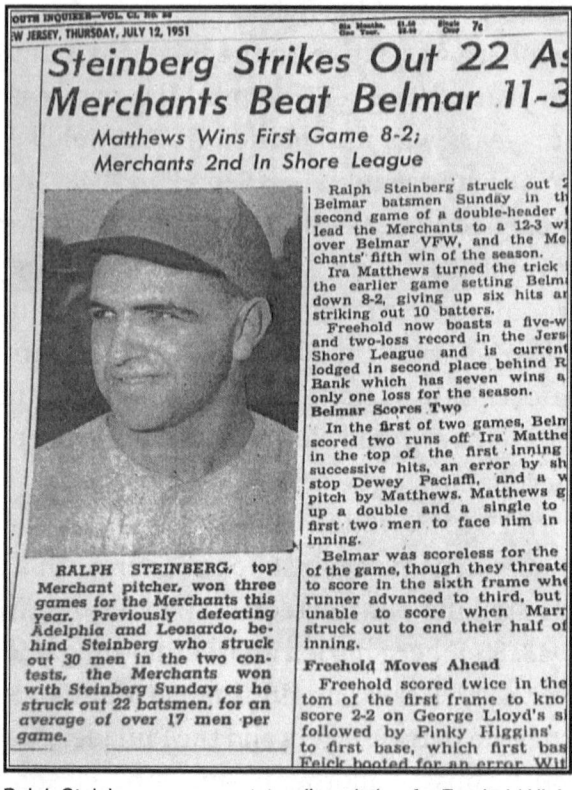

OUTH INQUIRER—VOL. CI, NO. 14
W JERSEY, THURSDAY, JULY 12, 1951

Steinberg Strikes Out 22 A: Merchants Beat Belmar 11-3

Matthews Wins First Game 8-2; Merchants 2nd In Shore League

Ralph Steinberg struck out 2 Belmar batsmen Sunday in th second game of a double-header t lead the Merchants to a 12-3 wi over Belmar VFW, and the Me chants' fifth win of the season.

Ira Matthews turned the trick the earlier game setting Belm: down 8-2, giving up six hits ar striking out 10 batters.

Freehold now boasts a five-w and two-loss record in the Jers; Shore League and is current lodged in second place behind R Bank which has seven wins a only one loss for the season.

Belmar Scores Two

In the first of two games, Belm scored two runs off Ira Matthe in the top of the first inning successive hits, an error by sh stop Dewey Paclaffi, and a w pitch by Matthews. Matthews g up a double and a single to first two men to face him in inning.

Belmar was scoreless for the of the game, though they threate to score in the sixth frame whe runner advanced to third, but unable to score when Marr struck out to end their half of inning.

Freehold Moves Ahead

Freehold scored twice in the tom of the first frame to kno score 2-2 on George Lloyd's si followed by Pinky Higgins' to first base, which first bas Feick booted for an error. Wit

RALPH STEINBERG, top Merchant pitcher, won three games for the Merchants this year. Previously defeating Adelphia and Leonardo, behind Steinberg who struck out 30 men in the two contests, the Merchants won with Steinberg Sunday as he struck out 22 batsmen, for an average of over 17 men per game.

Ralph Steinberg was an outstanding pitcher for Freehold High School and the Freehold Merchants. Courtesy of Steinberg archives

Steinberg joined the Freehold Merchants team and again narrowly missed another no-hitter in August 1950 as he struck out sixteen Leonardo players. Another first-inning single denied him the no-hitter. At this game, thanks to the influence of Cashion, Edith Houghton, the only woman scout in baseball at that time, was among the spectators.[50] Cashion knew Houghton well, as she had attempted to persuade him to join the Philly organization a few years earlier.

On July 4, 1951, while playing with the Freehold Merchants, Steinberg again faced Leonardo and again narrowly missed a no-hitter by a single in the last inning. He won the game 11–3 and struck out nineteen batters. Three days later, Steinberg beat Belmar 11–3 in the second game of a doubleheader. He amazingly struck out twenty-two batters in this game, allowing only two hits.[51]

Steinberg did sign a contract with the Chicago Cubs in August of 1951. However, he did not stay with the Cubs due to a salary dispute. Instead, he pursued the legal profession and became a distinguished judge in Florida, where he still resides.

On April 29, 2002, Judge Steinberg of the Hillsborough Circuit Court sentenced Darryl Strawberry to an eighteen-month prison term for violating his court-ordered parole. Strawberry was a seventeen-season major league baseball player on the World Series championship teams of the New York Mets in 1986 and the New York Yankees in 1996, 1998, and 1999.

Boys to Men

I would like to begin this 1950s decade by citing some good stats for my brother when he played for the Gulistan team early in the year. He clobbered three home runs in three games to set an unbroken Jersey Shore League record.[52]

The 1950 year-end Gulistans statistics released by Fred Rowe, business manager, showed Cashion as the big gun at the plate with a .311 average over their twenty-game season, Toon as the top hurler with a 4–0 record, and Ralph Steinberg with ninety-two strikeouts over his seven games of pitching.[53]

By 1950, the boys on the Freehold diamond were not boys. When Ralph Steinberg, Joe Rohm, and Ray Kuzava were on

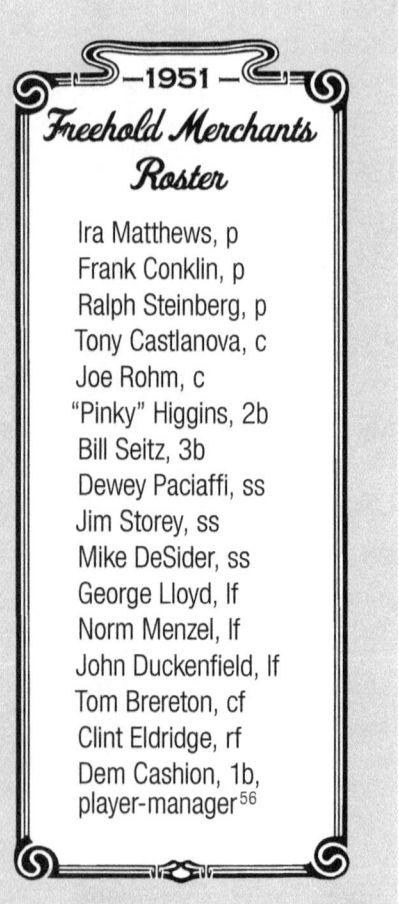

— 1951 —

Freehold Merchants Roster

Ira Matthews, p
Frank Conklin, p
Ralph Steinberg, p
Tony Castlanova, c
Joe Rohm, c
"Pinky" Higgins, 2b
Bill Seitz, 3b
Dewey Paciaffi, ss
Jim Storey, ss
Mike DeSider, ss
George Lloyd, lf
Norm Menzel, lf
John Duckenfield, lf
Tom Brereton, cf
Clint Eldridge, rf
Dem Cashion, 1b,
player-manager[56]

the field, the Gulistans were a tough nine. Dave Thompson had shed his "tools of ignorance" for an easier outfield spot. Cashion had lost some of his speed but would continue to hurl for another twenty-plus years.

Carl "Swede" Hansen was talking of retiring. Guggy Lewis retired, and he and Schanck were thinking about managing a group of local Black ball players. Marty Diggins went back to farming. Bill Tela was managing, and Joe McGlory had given up the game.[54] Charlie Malko had stated that the proliferation of television had hurt attendance. No longer did the Sunday games attract crowds of seven or eight hundred.[55]

Cashion couldn't sit back and see Freehold baseball become a historical footnote. He felt strongly that Freehold still had boys and men who wanted to enjoy the national pastime. Thus, in early 1950, Cashion proposed a team that would keep semipro baseball alive in Freehold.

He became the chief fundraiser, knocking on the doors of Main and South Street businesses. He received broad support from the local merchants and, appropriately, named the new team the Freehold Merchants. He also was able to utilize the equipment from the old Gulistans team.

The Freehold Merchants team was powered by the arm of Ralph Steinberg, as noted above. The team was a powerhouse for three seasons. Assisted by Guggy Lewis and Dick Skehan, Cashion managed successful seasons and enjoyed several very exciting games at the Lincoln Place field.

Another noteworthy team was put together in 1955 by the Freehold American Legion post and the Cameron-Roberson Agency; the team would play in the Monmouth Junior Baseball League. Cashion was the coach, along with Al Dangler. This team had a good balance of stellar pitchers in John McCarthy and Ed Ostrowski, coupled with the batting power of Roger Kane, Fred Quinn, and George Lott.

Other stellar Freehold picks included Butch Bennett, Joe

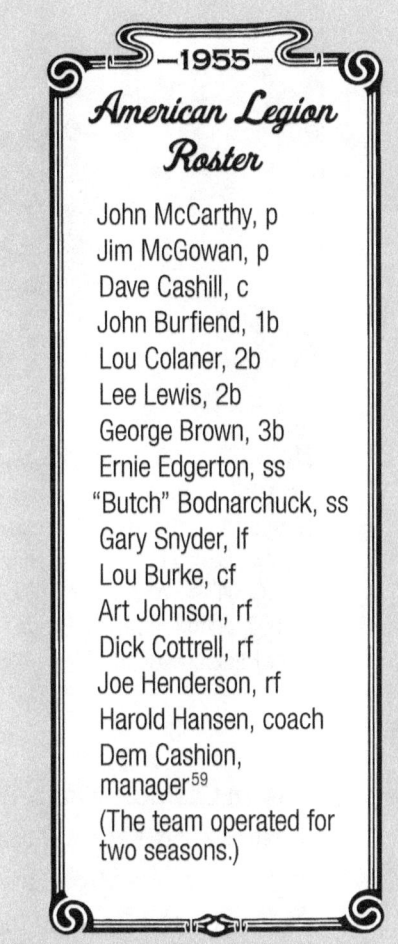

—1955—

American Legion Roster

John McCarthy, p
Jim McGowan, p
Dave Cashill, c
John Burfiend, 1b
Lou Colaner, 2b
Lee Lewis, 2b
George Brown, 3b
Ernie Edgerton, ss
"Butch" Bodnarchuck, ss
Gary Snyder, lf
Lou Burke, cf
Art Johnson, rf
Dick Cottrell, rf
Joe Henderson, rf
Harold Hansen, coach
Dem Cashion, manager[59]
(The team operated for two seasons.)

Henderson, John McCarthy, and John Burfiend.[57] During the previous Freehold High School baseball season, Ostrowski had hurled a perfect game against Neptune High School.[58]

In mid-April 1958, a committee was established to form a baseball club in Freehold. The committee members includ-

The 1958 Freehold Townsmen team had successful seasons through 1964. From left to right on the front row: Butch Bodnarchuck, John Duckenfield, Tom DeSalvo, Booby Quinn, Terry Hunt, Al VonSteenburg, Jack Tashjian. Second row: Dave Cashion, Walt Freeman, Ed Ostrowski, Roger Kane, Albie Prest, George Mitchell, John McCarthy, Bruce Phillips, Sid Blacknall, Porky Prest. Courtesy of Roger Kane collection

ed Dem Cashion, Warren "Porky" Prest, Ed Henderson, Dan Chestnut, Ed Feltus, Frank Witman, Joe Collins, and Lloyd Burlew. The Freehold Townsmen team had their first game, playing on the Freehold High School field, within a month.[60]

From 1958 through 1964, the Freehold Townsmen represented Freehold in the Jersey Shore Baseball League. Again, Cashion was the manager, as well as relief pitcher and first baseman. I remember this team well. There were some outstanding ball players on the Townsmen, and, while fans were sparse, the members of this team loved to play and they played well.

There was a little bit of everything during their eight-year run. There was great pitching, tremendous slug-

1958–1964
Freehold Townsmen Roster

Ed Ostrowski, p
Don Rooney, p
Ray Cosbar, p
John McCarthy, p
Lou Wells, p
Sid Blacknall, p
Don Cashion, p, lf
Ed Henderson, p, cf
Glenn Cashion, c
Bruce Phillips, c
Fred "Booby" Quinn, c
Walt Freeman, 1b
Howard Gerken, 1b
Al Von Steenburg, 1b
Wayne Cashion, 2b
Lou Mendini, 2b
Rich Kane, 2b
Gene Glum, 2b
Tommy George, ss, 2b
Terry Hunt, 2b, ss

Lloyd Burlew, 3b
Mickey Crawford, 3b
Albie Prest, 3b
George Mitchell, 3b
Tom DiSalvo, 3b
Roger Kane, ss
Tommy George, ss, 2b
Butch Bodnarchuck, lf
Bert Sathmery, lf
Art Spencer, lf
Harvey Whille, lf
Myron Van Cleaf, lf, 1b
George Lott, cf
John Duckenfield, cf
Frank Steinitz, rf
Joe Tomlinson, rf
Jack Tashjian, rf
Warren "Porky" Prest, coach
Dem Cashion, manager

ging, some antics on the field, and even a few baseball team brawls.

As the Freehold Townsmen reached their denouement on the diamond in 1964, Danny Lewis agreed to join the team. Lewis had been a Freehold High School football hero who went on to play in the National Football League from 1958 to 1966. He intended to play with the Townsmen until mid-July, when he would return to the Detroit Lions.

Lewis's signing completed the circle on Cashion's career. Lewis's father, Guggy Lewis, and Cashion had played together on the Freehold Holy Name team more than twenty-five years prior to this transaction. The Townsmen left the Freehold baseball fields at the end of 1964.

Finally! Little League Arrives

Before Little League became a significant element of Freehold baseball, there was a precursor called the Farm Belt League. In June of 1951, nearly six hundred boys eight to twelve years of age began playing in Monmouth County Little League baseball, organized by the Monmouth County Federation of Holy Name Societies.

Freehold's entrant in this league was the St. Rose of Lima team, which was managed by Ed Spuler. During the next two years, Cashion and Pinky Higgins would manage and coach this team.

Some of the players on St. Rose would transfer to the Freehold Little League, but a few of us remained with St. Rose. The St. Rose team competed in the Farm Belt League with the Englishtown Auctioneers, the Englishtown Farmers, St. Gabriel's in Bradevelt, and the Adelphia Blue Ball Bees.

The playing field of the St. Gabriel's team was at the Marlboro State Hospital. It was pretty interesting to be on the field and have the patients from the state hospital watching along the sidelines. Also, our youthful enthusiasm was always on display after winning an away game. We would pile into the back of Pinky Higgins's pickup truck and parade down Main Street in Freehold, yelling, "We won, we won, we won, by golly, we won!"

The town of Freehold went all out to form the Freehold Little League. Among the supporters of the league were the Blue and Gold Association, the Freehold Fire Department, the Square Club, the Local 26, the CIO, the United Textile Workers of America, the American Hotel, and the Rotary Club.

The Little League diamond was created on a field donated by Miss Lydia Parker. Parker donated the field with one stipulation—that there would be no Sunday ball playing. Leadership for the league's creation can be attributed to Bill Goldstein and Dick Skehan.

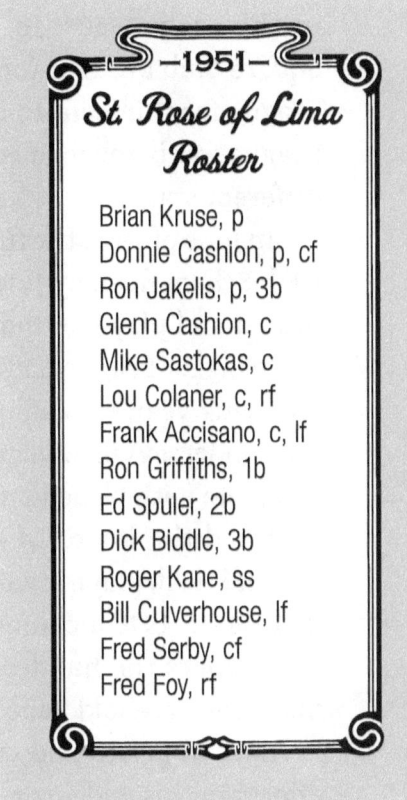

—1951—

St. Rose of Lima Roster

Brian Kruse, p
Donnie Cashion, p, cf
Ron Jakelis, p, 3b
Glenn Cashion, c
Mike Sastokas, c
Lou Colaner, c, rf
Frank Accisano, c, lf
Ron Griffiths, 1b
Ed Spuler, 2b
Dick Biddle, 3b
Roger Kane, ss
Bill Culverhouse, lf
Fred Serby, cf
Fred Foy, rf

On July 7, 1951, Parker Field was dedicated, with appropriate pomp and circumstance including the tossing of the first ball by Mayor Quinn, who exhibited some of his pitching prowess of the 1920s and 1930s. The Freehold Little League has continued unabated to this day. The only difference is that the players now play at the Wilson Community Park on Otterson Road in Freehold, named after longtime former mayor and Little League player Michael Wilson.

Organized youth baseball went beyond Little League in the early 1950s. In December of 1951, the Freehold Square Club brought forth the idea to start a Little Bigger League for thirteen- to fifteen-year-olds. The Little Bigger League was being formed in sixteen communities in eleven different states.

In June of 1952, the first game was played at the Freehold High School field. By July, Lincoln Place field had been renovated and play had moved to that diamond. By 1953, the Little Bigger League had become the Babe Ruth League. The following year, Nescafé provided space adjacent to its factory on Jerseyville Avenue to create an excellent ball field, complete with bleachers, dugouts, and a clubhouse.

I had the honor of scoring the first run on the new Nescafé field, playing with the championship Red Sox team in 1954. In 1976 a commemorative booklet was published that honors the hundreds of boys, men, and women who made the Freehold Babe Ruth League a success.

Special praise and credit go to the following for their efforts in this endeavor:

- E. I. Vanderveer, commissioner of the Little Bigger League
- Pete Vanderveer, president
- John Gutteridge, vice president
- Jack Steinberg, secretary
- Robert Guy, treasurer
- "Slim" McChesney, player-agent
- Dick Biddle, groundskeeper
- Ed Fountain, scorekeeper
- Tucker Potter, Dave McCallum, and Bill Freeman, Giants managers

- Louis Hantman, Bing Youmans, and Charlie Malekovich, Red Sox managers
- Dave Cashion and Tom Brereton, Braves managers
- Gene Evans and Norman Miles, Browns managers
- Bill Reardon, Ken Daley, and Hank Schanck, head umpires
- Scotty Carswell, Harvey Greenberg, Dewey Paciaffi, Sam McGackin, Ted Fountain, Ed Riddle, and Bill Fowler, umpires[61]

After I played on the St. Rose of Lima team and on the Red Sox in the Babe Ruth League, I was the catcher for Freehold High School and the Freehold Townsmen. Our high school had a decent team; however, we didn't lead the league during my four years.

I did manage to lead the league in batting in my senior year with a .441 average, as well as achieving All-Shore Conference and All-State recognition. During my four years at

Glenn Cashion was co-captain of the Brown University Baseball team in 1963. Courtesy of Cashion archives

Brown University, I started as a catcher, played first and right field for two seasons, and caught in my senior year. I had some good seasons, but nothing spectacular. Being elected co-captain of the team in my senior year was quite an honor.

Glenn Cashion is shown swinging for the fences at Brown University in 1963.
Courtesy of Cashion archives

A Decade of Pitching Prowess

I had a friend who was a big baseball player,
back in high school
He could throw that speedball by you,
make you look like a fool
Saw him the other night at this roadside bar,
I was walkin' in, he was walkin' out
We went back inside, sat down, had a few drinks,
but all he kept talking about was
Glory days, they'll pass you by
Glory days, in the wink of a young girl's eye
Glory days, glory days

"GLORY DAYS" BY BRUCE SPRINGSTEEN

During the decade of the 1950s, the strong pitching arms of young baseball players in Freehold Little League, Babe Ruth League, and Freehold High School were clearly in evidence. For example, my nephew, Donnie Cashion, pitched back-to-back no-hitters for St. Rose of Lima in 1951. Clearly he had learned a thing or two from his father, Dem.

This Johnny Vander Meer feat started a decade of fantastic pitching. Matching Cashion's two no-hitters were John McCarthy and "Lefty" Ed Ostrowski. Don Rooney hurled four no-hitters during his career in both leagues and in high school.

However, the most striking pitching accomplishment during that decade came from Jim "Leon" Mavroleon. In 1961, Leon pitched three no-hitters in Little League, including a Vander Meer feat, and ended his Little League career with six no-hitters.

Leon went to West Virginia University and threw another no-hitter for the Mountaineers. He was signed by the Cincinnati Reds and played two seasons of minor league ball. In total, during the decade of the 1950s, there were twenty-four no-hitters in Freehold Little League and Babe Ruth League and two in high school, for a total of twenty-six.

Dem's Last Season

Following the end of the Gulistan dynasty in Freehold baseball, Cashion was determined to keep baseball alive. He felt there were still a number of kids who wanted to play ball, and he was going to continue to be the guiding light.

In 1963 he teamed up with Abe Steinberg, owner of Freehold Furniture in Freehold, and they were able to start an Ed Carleton team in Freehold. Ron Udy, the high school baseball coach, was selected to manage the team. Tom Brereton, another old Gulistan ball player, would manage the team in later years.

In 1971, Cashion fostered a new Freehold team and so impressed the Jersey Shore League that the Freehold team was allowed to join the league in 1972. The pilot of this new team was, of course, Cashion, as player and coach.

On July 29, 1973, Freehold defeated Lincroft 11–9. In the third inning of this game, "Lincroft erupted for eight runs to knot the game at 9–9. Freehold took a two-run lead for good in the fourth on a two-run single by Dave Cashion."[62]

At the age of fifty-four, Cashion still had the batting eye and baseball savvy to win the ball game. That game was the last time Cashion's name was mentioned in Freehold box scores. His playing days were over. And his finale brings this century-plus history of Freehold baseball to a fitting close.

Next, we will take an in-depth look at my brother's life and explore his legendary prowess at our beloved national pastime.

"Well it's our game; that's the chief fact in connection with it: America's game; it has the snap, go, fling of the American atmosphere; it belongs as much to our institutions, fits into them as significantly as our Constitution's laws; is just as important in the sum total of our historic life."

—Walt Whitman

Chapter 6

DAVID "DEM" CASHION: ONE OF FREEHOLD'S BEST

The burden of good pitching. Curved or straight
Or in or out, or haply up or down,
To puzzle him that standeth by the plate,
To lessen, so to speak, his bat-renoun:
Like Christy Mathewson or Three-Fingered Brown,
So pitch that every man can but admire
And offer you the freedom of the town—
This is the end of every fan's desire.

—FRANKLIN PIERCE ADAMS

My brother, *David Eugene "Dem" Cashion, was a great pitcher* and could have become a prominent player in the major leagues. He was loved by fellow ball players, friends, and, of course, family. And like all of us, he was not perfect and certainly faced his fair share of stress in life. This narrative is his story, as viewed through my prism.

Dem's Formative Years

On Friday, December 20, 1918, Jane Cashion gave birth to a baby boy at Monmouth Memorial Hospital, Long Branch, New Jersey. While he was born into a family whose baseball

Dave "Dem" Cashion with the 1949 Kingston Colonials in the Eastern Shore League. Courtesy of Cashion archives

My brother, David Eugene Cashion (1918–1975), was a pitching standout, a solid first baseman, and a first-rate umpire. Courtesy of Cashion archives

roots go back to the late 1800s, no one could have foreseen the baseball exploits that Cashion would achieve or the fundamental principles of the game that he would instill in the hearts of thousands of Freehold baseball players. Cashion's great-uncle, Tony McNicholas, had pitched baseball nines to victory through the 1880s to the early 1900s.

Jane's husband, David Demarest Cashion, had been an outstanding catcher on the local Freehold baseball teams during the early 1900s. He had just about reached the end of his playing career when his son was born, and he was about to embark on an illustrious career of umpiring throughout the Freehold and Central Jersey environs. Both David Demarest and his brother, Edward Casper, were managers of the local Freehold team early in the 1900s.

Jane brought her son, David Eugene, to her home on Court Street, which was across from the Monmouth Court House.

As was typical with the Cashion family, their stay at the Court Street residence was of short duration. Financial concerns motivated the nomadic existence of the Cashion/McNicholas families; they were constantly moving from house to house throughout Freehold. There were only two households with family ties for long periods. The first was 27 McLean Street, purchased by Jane in August 1941, shortly after the death of her husband David Demarest on July 6, 1941.

The other long-standing family domicile was 87 Randolph Street, purchased by John Fitzgibbon, the husband of Ann Garrity, in 1858. That site housed the following families: Fitzgibbon, Farrell, Garrity, Fallon, McNicholas, Haggarity, and Springsteen.

Why is he called "Dem" rather than "Dave"? He was called Dave by some; however, the vast majority of folks called him Dem. Sometimes "Dem" was morphed into

"Dim." According to local legend, the nickname came from local sportswriters who said his fastball used to fog past the batters.[1]

Although he was never known for his speed on the base paths, his fastball did have heavy velocity and was described as an "aspirin tablet streaking by." The more common explanation is that his father, David Demarest, was nicknamed "Dem."

Sadly, there isn't much documentation available for my brother's early childhood, although I am aware of several traumatic events in our family that certainly impacted him. In 1927, when Cashion was nine, his six-year-old cousin, Virginia Springsteen, was killed in a tragic truck accident. Virginia's parents, Fred and Alice Springsteen, were so distraught by the fatal accident that they could not adequately care for their three-year-old son, Douglas. Thus, my mother took Douglas into her home for approximately three years.

Another sad day for the family was October 25, 1926, when our grandfather, Edward Cashion, died.

Tragedy struck again in 1931 when our six-year-old sister, Ann, was struck by an automobile. She sustained a fractured skull and deep lacerations on the right side of her forehead. She remained unconscious for several hours, but eventually made a complete recovery.

Cashion was one of twenty-two graduates from St. Rose of Lima grammar school in June of 1933. He then spent short stints at Freehold High School and St. James High School in Red Bank, New Jersey, but never graduated from high school.

During his short-lived high school days, he was on the freshman football team, was an officer in the local Boys Glee Club and boxed under the guidance of Mickey Walker (World Welterweight Champion, 1922; World Middleweight

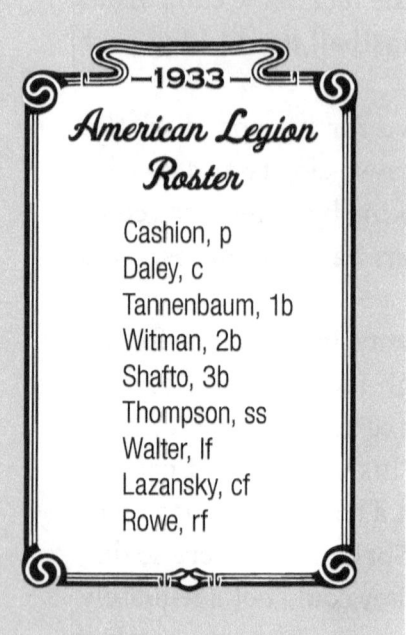

—1933 —
American Legion Roster

Cashion, p
Daley, c
Tannenbaum, 1b
Witman, 2b
Shafto, 3b
Thompson, ss
Walter, lf
Lazansky, cf
Rowe, rf

Champion, 1926).[2] During the early 1930s, my father donned his old catcher's mitt and spent many hours catching with Dem.

Cashion's pitching prowess developed quickly. In 1936, when he was just eighteen, he was offered a tryout with the Newark Bears of the minor league International League.[3] From 1932 to 1950, the Bears were the top club in the New York Yankees farm system. The 1932 team, with a record of 109 wins and 59 losses, won the Little World Series Championship. The team's roster included fourteen men who went on to play in the majors, including Red Rolfe and Dixie Walker.[4] Cashion performed admirably during the tryout and almost made the team, but his youth was a detriment.

During the mid-1930s, Cashion began his meteoric rise to pitching fame, while also playing first base when not on the "pitcher's box," as it was called in the late nineteenth century.[5] Cashion's batting was also a key element of his baseball success—an ability he maintained long after his pitching days had ended.

Cashion's first recorded game was in June of 1933, playing with a Freehold American Legion, Post 54, team against Lakewood. Freehold lost the game, although David Cashion, local twirler, pitched out fifteen men.[6]

Cashion's next outing as a pitcher was in July with the Freehold Firemen's team. For the next three decades, he played for several local teams. Where there was a need for a good pitcher, Cashion was actively recruited. On that July day with the Firemen's team, he was the winning pitcher, striking out fourteen men and hitting a three-bagger. A week later, Cashion rejoined the Legion team and struck out more than half of the outs of the game, with sixteen strikeouts. To top it off, he hit a home run in that game.

In 1934, Cashion "pitched out 17 men" at a game against the Hightstown American Legion team. "Dem has pitched in three games this season, two of which were with Farmingdale. Both games were of five-inning duration, and he pitched out 5 in the first game and 9 in the second. With his 17 strikeouts last night, he has 31 strikeouts to his credit."[7]

Always on the Field

Cashion seemed to be playing ball constantly during the mid-1930s. He continued to play with the Legion team, winning the Shore Conference Championship in 1936. While playing for them, Cashion set a Legion record with eighteen strikeouts in a seven-inning game. He also donned the uniform of the Cubs, Indians, Englishtown Sporting Club, Freehold Firemen, and Red Bank Pirates, demonstrating his baseball versatility by playing shortstop with the Cardinals and center field with the Firemen.

However, Cashion's primary team during this period, continuing to 1940, was the Freehold Holy Name team. His pitching and hitting skills led the Holy Name team to numerous wins and championships.

On July 4, 1935, the Holy Name team beat the Raritan A.C. Colored Players by a score of 9-5. While this marked the first encounter Cashion had against a Black baseball team, he subsequently played on several teams who played great games against outstanding Black teams from various New Jersey and New York towns.

The 1935 year-end statistics for the Holy Name team show Cashion's batting average as .322. "The club registered defeats against such strong teams as the Footes A.C. of Manalapan who won 14 straight victories; and the Freehold Firemen's nine, who won the second half of the County League Championship. Percy Anderson piloted the team through their impressive season of victories."[8]

The Holy Name team dominated the sporting headlines, with frequent "Cashion" mentions during this period. Among the highlights was a game against Nutley in 1937 in which Cashion recorded fifteen strikeouts. Another noteworthy game was in May 1937. Holy Name lost this game to Keyport 4–3, but Cashion pitched admirably with twelve strikeouts. What is memorable about this outing is that the man who called the game was Dem's father, in one of his last appearances as an umpire.[9]

During the winter months, Cashion needed some other athletic pursuit, so he formed the Shore Basketball League and figured prominently in many wins for the Freehold basketball team. For example, in 1936, the Freehold team knocked off a good Point Pleasant team 47–46, with Cashion as the high scorer with twenty points.

Tragedy struck our family again in 1936 when my mom gave birth to a "blue baby" on December 20. Unfortunately, Richard, the baby boy, lived for only three days. Our family was understandably devastated by the loss.

Cashion's first baseball contract, signed on May 8, 1937, was with the Sayreville National Lead Company team in the

The 1937 National Lead Championship team, Central Jersey Industrial League, included Dave Cashion (top row, third from left) and Hank Schanck (top row, fifth from left). Courtesy of Cashion archives

Middlesex County Industrial League. The press release stated, "Dave Cashion, ace right-hander of the Freehold Holy Name baseball club, signed a contract on Saturday . . . Percy Anderson, manager of the local Holy Name team, accompanied Cashion and witnessed the contract signing. The Industrial League, which plays four games a week, will use Cashion during the week days. His services to the Holy Name team, thus, will not be lost for Sunday games."[10]

Cashion did indeed continue to excel with Holy Name. He went 4 for 5 at bat, striking out eleven, in a win over Union Beach in July of 1937.

My brother's success with the National Lead team in 1937 led them to first place in the Industrial League of Middlesex County. "Youthful Dave Cashion, one of the hardest working semipro pitchers in this area, gained a measure of the recognition due him. He led the National Lead nine to first place in the Industrial League of Middlesex County. In addition, Cashion was credited with winning the two final games that captured the Loop title."

A newspaper of that locality shows "Cashion a dependable hurler and handler of a wicked bat . . . At this point, Cashion, who had gone in to hurl the last two frames, stepped up to the plate and promptly drove out a single. That sent the winning run over the plate and wound up the series in favor of the Leaders. Cashion has been working on the mound for several years, despite his youth, seeing action with the Holy Namers, local Firemen, and Englishtown Sporting Club. He plays a bang-up game at first base also."[11]

Hall of Famer Willie Stargell (left field, Pittsburgh Pirates) is famously quoted as comparing a knuckleball to a butterfly with hiccups, and Cashion had a good one.

According to Cashion's wife, Betty, his tenure with the National Lead team precipitated his famous and frightening knuckleball. Cashion had injured his finger, so it was slightly misaligned and therefore allowed for a novel grip for his knuckleball.[12]

There is, however, another theory about the development of his knuckleball. A sportswriter had opined that Cashion was taught the pitch by Paul Schreiber, who had hurled briefly for the New York Yankees and the Brooklyn Dodgers.[13] Cashion met Schreiber during his stint with the Belmar Braves. I favor the more authoritative view of his wife.

No-No

Every pitcher dreams of a no-hitter, and Cashion achieved this major milestone on June 12, 1937, when the Freehold Firemen beat Atlas A.C. of Long Branch. Our dad was the ump for this game. Incredibly, Cashion pitched a one-hitter the very next day.[14]

Indeed, my brother prized these exploits. When asked to fill out a William J. Weiss Baseball Statistics questionnaire in August 1949, Cashion listed those two games as his answer to the question, "What would you consider your most interesting or unusual experience in baseball?"[15]

Cashion's first recorded game with the Gulistans, sponsored by the A. & M. Karagheusian rug mill, was in July of 1938. It was a state tournament game, played at Dunn Field in Trenton. After giving up three runs in the sixth inning in one of his rare subpar performances, he left the game.

However, there would be many brighter moments for Cashion and the Gulistans in future years. My brother rebounded from this defeat with a resounding win while playing with the Englishtown Sporting Club against the highly touted Belmar Braves in September of 1938. Cashion's bat came to life and he pounded out three extra-base hits in four trips to the plate, and his team won 10–5.

In October 1938, at the age of nineteen, Cashion signed a contract to play with the Salisbury, Maryland, baseball team of the Eastern Shore League. This team was owned by the Washington Senators. Records at the Hall of Fame in Cooperstown show contractual activity with Salisbury in February of 1939.[16]

Cashion was ordered to report to the spring training camp in St. Augustine, Florida, on March 16. However, he did not arrive until mid-1940 due to pressing family matters, including his recent marriage and the birth of his first son (David Donald, born in November of 1939).

Cashion's pitching prominence with the Freehold Gulistans continued until he eventually departed for the

Salisbury team. On April 30, 1939, he shut out the Riverdale Field Club 2–0. Two weeks later, he led the Gulistans to a 5–3 win over the House of David, striking out thirteen.

He ended the month of May with a sparkling pitching performance against Plainfield. The Gulistans won 8–0, with Cashion striking out sixteen and giving up a paltry three hits.

My brother married Elizabeth Murphy on July 2, 1939, at the St. Rose of Lima Church. The couple lived with her parents at 95 Parker Street, the first of eight homes in which they would reside.[17]

The Cashions were a handsome couple. Murphy had recently graduated from high school and was a Freehold beauty who always looked good. Every time I saw her, she was well-dressed with her hair in perfect place. She was even dressed to the nines when she watched her husband play and manage teams.

There was a photo of her and her firstborn, Don, in the window of McKelvey's furniture store on Main Street in 1940, as the youngest mother in Freehold. My brother was the pride of Freehold, a good-looking guy with a wonderfully warm personality and already one of Freehold's greatest athletes.

Cashion was quick to get back into action with the Gulistans. In a couple of clashes with Englishtown Sporting Club in August of 1939, he overwhelmed his opponent, winning the first game 7–2 and the second 9–5. In this encounter, Cashion had thirteen strikeouts and hit a blistering triple to assist in the team's victory.

Due to Cashion's pitching prowess, he was signed with the Washington Senators to play for its Salisbury franchise in the Eastern Shore League. However, we will never clearly understand the saga of his entrance into this franchise. His

My brother Dem and his wife Betty Cashion, c. 1943. Courtesy of Cashion archives

family life certainly played a role in his reluctance to move ahead with the contractual arrangements.

The following news release of January 1940 details the situation: "Johnny Calandriello of Red Bank received a letter from Charlie Draper, scout of the Springfield club of the Eastern Baseball league, yesterday. It revealed that "Dim" Cashion of Freehold is still the property of the Salisbury club of the Eastern Shore loop (Class D) and that the husky young right-hand flinger would report to Salisbury this Spring or else be suspended. Cashion has agreed to report for spring training as soon as notified to leave Freehold, which will probably be around the middle of March. Johnny Calandriello is a shore representative for certain minor league clubs."[18]

Cashion did not take any action as a result of the letter. In an apparent plea to start his minor league career with the Dodgers, the following news release of May 1940 is of interest: "Dim Cashion and Andy McGackin motored to Ebbets Field yesterday morning for a conference with Larry McPhall and manager Leo Durocher of the Brooklyn Dodgers. Cashion is under contract with the Salisbury club of the Eastern Shore League but refused to report this spring and was suspended. Cashion must report to that club, and then a deal may be arranged to sell or trade him to a Brooklyn Dodger farm team."[19]

My brother did join the Salisbury club in July 1940, but not before a couple of final local games. First, he led the Holy Namers to a 14–1 win over Hopelawn A.A. in early June as a gesture to his long association with the team. This win kept the undefeated season alive for the Holy Name club.

In June, Cashion joined the Red Bank Pirates to play against the Newark Eagles at the Newman Springs field in Red Bank, the site of numerous games between the Freehold and Red Bank teams up through the 1960s. The Newark Eagles were members of the National Negro League, and one of the team members was Monte Irvin, who would join the New York Giants in 1949.

Tryout Tales

In an *Asbury Park Press* article in July of 1940, Herb Kamm relates that Cashion went to a Cleveland Indians tryout in Belmar in May during his period of being AWOL from the Salisbury team. The person in charge of the tryout was Charlie Draper, formerly of the Washington Senators.

"Dave turned up under an assumed name, but Draper remembered his face. 'You're Dave Cashion from Freehold, the boy I signed up last year for Salisbury, aren't you? . . . Why didn't you report?' And Cashion went on to explain that he didn't feel he could make the grade, didn't want to give up a steady job in Freehold—and didn't want to leave home and his friends. Draper explained to Cashion that he was bound by that contract and, while he would like to sign him up with Cleveland, he couldn't. At the urging of Draper and his friends, Dave left for Salisbury last week. Dave had a job at the rug mill, and the firm was kind enough to give him a leave of absence until the Eastern Shore league season is over. Dave's friends also came through—a couple of days after his departure, the boys got together, made a collection for him, and sent him a nice bundle of cash—just a token of esteem."[20]

Press reports of Cashion's performance while at Salisbury include these notes:

"He hung up the tourney strikeout record in winning his first start."[21]

"Dave 'Dim' Cashion, a husky right-handed knuckleball hurler from Freehold, is turning in impressive mound performances since he joined the Salisbury club of the Eastern Shore League over eight weeks ago."[22]

"Dave Cashion continues to do himself proud down with the Salisbury, MD club in the Eastern Shore League. He won a 12–3 decision, lost a 3–2 verdict, and had a no-decision in three innings of relief hurling in another tussle [sic]. Cashion is enjoying organized ball, which will come

as quite a surprise to many of his Freehold friends who were afraid that Dim would become homesick and jump the team. Dave also says the loop is very fast and the competition keen. Keep up the good work, Dave, and your pals will do you proud on your return to the County seat."[23]

"Information trickling out of Freehold reveals that Dave Cashion, former Freehold Holy Name twirler, who is well-known to every semipro ball player in the County, enjoyed a successful season with Salisbury in the Eastern Shore League. Cashion appeared in 11 games with Salisbury during the regular season, pitching 59 innings, and is credited with four victories and three defeats for a pitching record of .571. Incidentally, Salisbury captured the league title in a playoff with Milford."[24]

Upon Cashion's return from Salisbury, a game was played to honor the twenty-one-year-old baseball star. Everyone in Freehold considered him a hero. He had made it to the minor leagues! After that, who knew what was in his future?

"The October 6, 1940, game, played at the Institute Place, pitted the Holy Namers against the Freehold All-Stars. Cashion was the designated pitcher for the Holy Name team, and Percy Anderson was the manager. John Palladino Sr. of the Englishtown Sporting Club managed the All-Stars, who came from the Cubs, Cosmos, and Eagles of Freehold and the Englishtown club.

"The All-Stars roster included Herb Layton, Dan Federici, Vincent Bellamy, and Joseph Spevak of the Cubs; Gilbert Toon, Joseph Daily, William Wilson, and George MacMahon

ALL-STAR GAME TO HONOR CASHION

Will Play Holy Name Team On Sunday

Plans were completed this week for the Holy Name-All Star baseball game to be played next Sunday afternoon on the Lincoln Place diamond. The game, which will begin at 2 o'clock, is being played to honor Dave Cashion, who recently returned from the training camp of the Indians baseball team at Salisbury, Maryland. He will be presented with a gift at home plate, during the game.

John Palladino, Sr., of the Englishtown Sporting Club will manage the All Stars, composed of representatives of the Cubs, Cosmos, and Eagles, of Freehold; and the Englishtown club. He will be assisted by Leon Weinstein, manager of the Cosmos; and Harry Jackson, manager of the Eagles.

Cashion will pitch for the Holy Name team, and Manager Percy Anderson expects to keep his original line-up intact.

The All-Stars will be composed of Herbert Layton, Dan Federici, Vincent Bellamy, and Joseph Spevak, of the Cubs; Gilbert Toon, Joseph Dailey, William Wilson, and George MacMahon, of the Cosmos; Henry Neiberlein, Warren Prest, John Palladino, Jr., and Harry Narazonick, of the E. S. C.; George Emmons, Joseph Conover, "Lick" Robinson, and Sammy Stiles, of the Eagles.

Freehold held a Dave Cashion Day for my brother in October of 1940. Courtesy of Cashion archives

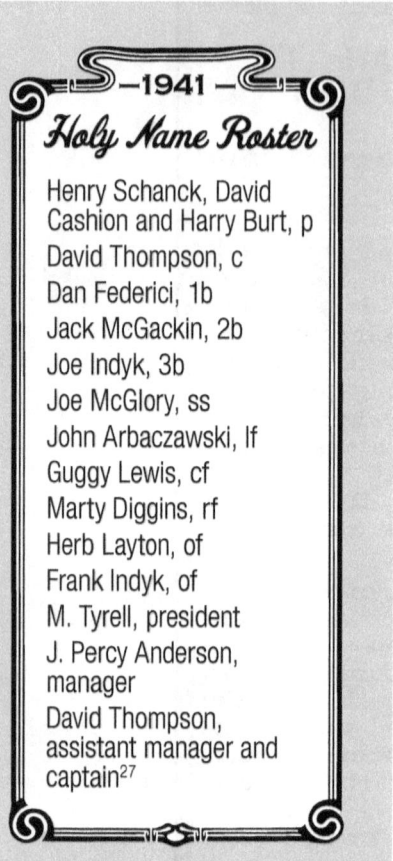

of the Cosmos; John Palladino Jr. and Harry Narazonick of the E.S.C; and George Emmons, Joe Conover, "Lick" Robinson, and Sammy Stiles of the Eagles."[25]

As the story should rightly unfold, Cashion hurled a masterful game. He tossed a three-hitter and struck out eleven. The Holy Name gang won the game 4–1. "At the end of the game, Dem was presented a gift by Percy Anderson of the Holy Name."[26]

If I do say so myself, another key date in Cashion's life was when I came along. I was born on December 29, 1940, and they named me Robert Glenn, although I would go by my middle name as per family tradition.

In 1941, my brother returned to playing with the Holy Name club. Why he didn't return to Salisbury is unknown. It is safe to speculate that he felt more comfortable staying at home. He was recently married and raising a young boy. He didn't lack any playing skills, as he demonstrated over the next few months. Behind Cashion's right arm and mighty bat, the Holy Name club had an outstanding year in 1941.

Before the climactic end of the 1941 Holy Name season, Cashion played in an All-Star game at Belmar on May 30,

Henry Schanck, David Cashion and Harry Burt, p
David Thompson, c
Dan Federici, 1b
Jack McGackin, 2b
Joe Indyk, 3b
Joe McGlory, ss
John Arbaczawski, lf
Guggy Lewis, cf
Marty Diggins, rf
Herb Layton, of
Frank Indyk, of
M. Tyrell, president
J. Percy Anderson, manager
David Thompson, assistant manager and captain[27]

1941. The twenty-three players selected represented the best of Monmouth and Ocean counties, matched against the tough Belmar Braves team.

Kamm of the *Asbury Park Press* reported, "The star of the Belmar Braves-Shore All-Stars baseball game was Dave Cashion . . . Belmar scored six runs in the seventh, but they were a series of bad breaks and mushy base hits. In other words, Dave was not belted out of the box and, with better luck, he would have been around at the finish ...Whitey Dreesin, the Braves Manager, recognized this and said, 'This boy Cashion is all right. I liked the way he handled himself out there, and he seemed to have plenty on the ball. From what I saw, I couldn't tell much about the others, but Cashion looks like he'll do.' Dreesin was a bit more impressed when told that Dave worked for a spell with Salisbury in the Eastern Shore League."[28]

The news quickly spread that "Dave Cashion, young Freehold pitching star, will make his first appearance in a Belmar Braves uniform, at Belmar, Friday night when the Brooklyn Royal Giants tackle the Braves in a game that is scheduled for 9:00 PM. Cashion pitched brilliantly for the Monmouth-Ocean All-Stars against the Braves in the opening game at Memorial Field, thus earning the opportunity to show his wares in a Belmar uniform."[29]

Cashion was the winning pitcher in a Belmar win over the Detroit Clowns on June 20, 1941, although he didn't pitch up to his potential. He had been scheduled to pitch against the Newark Eagles a few days before the Clowns game, but our father had a major operation at Long Branch Hospital that afternoon. Unfortunately, our dad never left the hospital. He died of post-operation complications on July 6, 1941.

Tragic Blow

My father's death left a massive wound in my brother's heart. How much this contributed to future psychological issues is unclear, but it most likely was a significant factor. At this time, Dem, his wife Betty, and Donnie lived with Betty's parents on Parker Street. My mother and I were at 37 McLean Street. My mother had resumed working for the telephone company, and I was cared for by my grandmother, Jennie McNicholas. Ultimately, my mother was able to get a mortgage from the local savings and loan company and purchased a house at 27 McLean Street. While these issues were not my brother's responsibility, I do wonder how much our mother's plight weighed on him.

My brother continued to play with both the Belmar Braves and Holy Name for the rest of 1941. The Holy Name team had an outstanding season and qualified to go against Point Pleasant in a three-game playoff for the league championship. Cashion's pitching had greatly aided the club's run to the playoffs; however, he became the first baseman during the homestretch.

I speculate that he had lost a bit of mental focus during this time. However, he never lost his batting eye. The Holy Name team won the first playoff game 2–1. They lost the second playoff game 7–6. In the final playoff game, Cashion "hammered out two singles and a double for the Holy Name to help lead the batting attack," and they won the league championship by a score of 6–2.[30]

The period from 1942 to 1943 is a quiet time in Cashion's baseball life, perhaps due to family issues. Betty gave birth to another boy, Richard Wayne, on January 16, 1943. In early 1944, Dem, Betty, Donnie, and Wayne moved to 39½ Institute Street. They would remain there for the next ten years, until another branch of the family, the Springsteens, moved there.

The Institute Street home was a small, four-room house with no hot water, but it was home to my brother's family and the site of numerous birthday parties and family gatherings. I saw my first professional football game on TV at their house. Our sister, Ann, and her husband, Richie, used to save their quarters and go to Dem's house to enjoy their coin-operated TV. One quarter inserted in the coin slot provided one hour of TV viewing.

In August 1944, our mom remarried. Her new husband, Patsy Meo, owned the Blue Moon Inn, a well-known tavern and restaurant in Farmingdale, New Jersey. Meo would invest heavily to modernize the 27 McLean Street residence. The Blue Moon Inn would be the site of the wedding reception of Adele and Doug Springsteen in 1948. Dem was the best man for his cousin Doug.

My brother was called to military service, along with several men from Freehold. He left for the Army on May 23, 1944, and his discharge came on March 17, 1946. During his time in the Army, he did play service baseball.

He was initially sent to Fort Custer, Michigan, and played under player-coach Peanuts Lowrey, who later would compile a .273 batting average with several major league clubs. His following assignments were at Camp Robinson in Arkansas and then Hawaii before he boarded a ship for the South Pacific. While in Honolulu, Cashion played with Ted Williams and Billy Herman.[31]

The USS *Bergen* (APA–150) was my brother's duty ship during his Far East tenure. The USS *Bergen* had joined the Pacific fleet in December of 1944 and had shuttled troops and cargo from the West Coast to Pearl Harbor and Saipan (March 2–July 4, 1945).

She departed Pearl Harbor on July 11, landed her passengers at Okinawa on August 12, and then left for Inchon,

Korea, on September 5 with occupation troops. Leaving Okinawa again on September 26, the USS *Bergen* carried troops to China and returned to San Francisco, arriving on November 20. She made another trip to the Philippines (December 7, 1945, to January 24, 1946) to bring home returning servicemen. Decommissioning of the USS *Bergen* occurred on April 24, 1946.[32]

The mental lapses that had diminished my brother's repertoire on the field vanished when he returned to the mound at the Lincoln Place field in May 1946. The Gulistans were going against the always tough Belmar Braves; the Gulistans had beaten the strong Red Bank Towners the week before and were anxious to continue their winning ways.

Prior to the war, the fans came out by the hundreds—sometimes as many as a thousand—to watch the local players. Young and old would watch; some sat on the low bleacher behind the home plate screen, but most would sit along the first and third base sidelines.

The "concession stand" was a tub of iced soda. A player gave up his hat to be passed among the fans for the day's collection of coins during the game. The collection would be distributed among the team. Children hung out around the bleachers, on the ready to race down the Hull Avenue hill to retrieve foul balls. If they were lucky, a player would reward them with a quarter.

My brother was in command throughout the game. The fans remembered honoring him in October of 1940 and knew that he had a 12–3 record with the Salisbury Indians. His fastball was whistling by the batters; his curveball was falling off the cliff as the batters swung at it. However, his most frustrating pitch was his tantalizing knuckleball, which denied even the best hitters a decent swing.

The game ended with a 12–1 victory for the home team. The next day, local folks said, "That Cashion, he'll get signed yet if he keeps playing like that."[33]

No doubt Cashion's skills were legendary. But were they enough to get him to the bigs?

Chapter 7

DAVID "DEM" CASHION:
HE LIVED IT UNTIL THE END

Now we will delve into Cashion's tryouts, get a glimpse of his likable personality, witness his prowess in a number of positions, and see how he was a tireless advocate for Freehold baseball.

For the remainder of 1946 through April of 1948, Cashion continued to lead the Gulistan club to winning seasons. However, in September of 1946, he almost became a member of the Philadelphia Phillies franchise when he decided to go for a tryout. By this time, his contractual relationship with the Salisbury Indians had ended.

My brother reminisced about his tryout in a *Freehold Transcript* (our weekly newspaper) article some years ago:

"It was quite an eventful day for me. I went down to Philly with a catcher from Point Pleasant. No one was on the field when we arrived, so we went into the clubhouse. We waited for 20 minutes, and no one showed up. Then, finally, I see this guy who looks like a custodian. 'Hey, mack,'

I hollered. 'Where do we get some lockers?' He pointed to a locker and said to use that one over there. Then Schoolboy Rowe, who I'd recognize anywhere, comes in and yells something like, 'Hey, Ennis.' Then it comes to me. Here I was talking to Del Ennis as if he were the janitor." [Ennis had a major league average of .284 and socked 288 home runs.] "Naturally," Cashion continued, "I apologized to him. And you know what he said, 'It doesn't make any difference. I've been hitting like the janitor all spring anyway.'"

After getting a locker, Cashion went out in the field to pitch to Philadelphia catcher Rollie Hemsley. "I was throwing the knuckler, and it was working pretty good. But little did I know that the coach looking me over, Sy Perkins, can't stand knuckleball pitchers. He came over to me and told me to try other pitches besides the knuckler, but I tried to tell him that the knuckler was my best pitch. He just turned and walked away. I was greatly discouraged, but a man leaning on a stand called me over to him. It was Herb Pennock, the former Yankee pitcher who was then General Manager of the Phillies. He explained to me that Perkins once got his hand broken by a knuckleball pitcher and has hated every one of them since then. Pennock told me, 'I think you can get somebody out in his league. How would you like to give it a try at Wilmington, Delaware [then Class B]?'"[1]

The Phillies franchise tried to convince my brother to sign with them. Betty, his wife, told me that one Philly scout in particular was after Dem's signature. This determined scout was Edith Houghton. The *New York Times* reported, "There had only been one other female scout in baseball history, Bessie Largent, who with her husband, Roy, had acted as a scouting team from 1925–1943. Edith was, therefore, the second female scout in baseball history, and she was acting alone. She was hired in 1946, and for nearly 65 years after Houghton left baseball in 1951, not a single woman, it appears, worked for a M.L.B. team as a full-time scout. Numerous females were part-time, or "bird-dog," scouts, but not full time.

"At ten years old, Houghton had ranked among the United States' best female baseball players, and she had toured Japan in the 1920s with the Philadelphia Bobbies. Later she played with the New York Bloomer Girls and the Hollywood Girls, two of the top women's barnstorming teams. She also served in WAVES, the women's division of the United States Navy. Finally, in 1946, with her playing career over, Houghton approached Phillies owner Robert Carpenter and talked her way into a job as a full-time scout.

"During her five-plus years with the Phillies, Houghton reportedly signed 16 players, none reaching the majors. She was recalled back into the Navy in 1951."[2]

Houghton badgered Cashion in 1946 to sign with the Phillies. In September, there was an erroneous press release referencing the fact that "Dave (Dim) Cashion, Freehold ace, has signed with the Philadelphia Phillies for spring training."[3] Dem never signed with the Phillies, and he continued to play for the Gulistans until his next minor league stint.

Banner Years

For Cashion and the Gulistans, 1946 and 1947 were banner years. In the first home game of 1946, Cashion carried the team to a 12–1 thrashing of the highly touted Belmar Braves. On August 11, 1946, he set a Jersey Shore Baseball League record by recording seventeen strikeouts against Keyport at the Freehold High School baseball field. Besides pitching flawlessly, Cashion also scored the tying run in the fifth inning and the winning run in the sixth.

GULISTAN A.A.'S IN ACTION

This 1946 photo shows Dem blasting a home run for the Gulistans and Bill Tela showing his pitching form. Courtesy of Monmouth County Historical Association

Cashion's record that season was 15–2. For most of the season, the Gulistans were on top of the league. They finally succumbed to the Red Bank Towners, who beat them in a two-out-of-three playoff series.[4]

In 1947, the Gulistans continued their torrid winning ways. Early in the season, against the hometown rival, the Freehold A.C.s, the Gulistans won 8–4. In this encounter, the winning pitcher was Swede Hansen, known for his batting skills, and Cashion played a restful right field. Again, my brother's bat was conspicuous, leading the ten-hit attack with a home run and a single.

I should note that the Jersey Shore Baseball League in this period consisted of two divisions. The American Division included Keyport, Long Branch, Gulistans, Port Monmouth, Red Bank Towers, Red Bank Braves, Point Pleasant, and Belmar. The National Division included Lakewood, Tinton Falls, West Belmar, Asbury Park, Freehold A.C., Cliffwood, Vail Homes, and Matawan.

The Gulistan club not only had Cashion's pitching that year; they had overall team batting power. On May 11, 1947, in a contest against Keyport, the mighty Gulistans went on a twenty-hit, twenty-run rampage and won the game 20–5, with my brother as the winning pitcher. On August 24, 1947, Cashion pitched four-hit ball against Port Monmouth and coasted to an overwhelming 19–0 triumph. Cashion ended the season with an 11–3 record.

The National Division League two-out-of-three playoff matched the Gulistans against Keyport. In the first match, the thrilling game went twelve innings. It was 1–1 at the end of nine innings. "Cashion calmed the Keyport Legion with a half-dozen safeties . . . Cashion also rapped the Keyport pitcher for a pair of safeties."[5]

The National Division Championship came on September 7, 1947, with a 5–3 win, with Hansen driving in all five runs and Cashion getting the win.

The Little World Series of the Jersey Shore League pitted the Gulistans against Asbury Park. The first game, at the Lincoln Street field, was a sight to behold. "A crowd of approximately 1,000 people saw the Asbury Park nine recover from a six-inning 3–2 deficit to tie the count in the ninth. The Gulistans had matched the Asbury Park nine's tallies in the first and went ahead 3–2 on Cashion's homer over the left-field fence in the second, bounced back to win the game in the lower half of the ninth when Lewis walked, moved to second on McGackin's infield out and scored on a slashing single by Dan Federici, to win the contest 4–3, with Cashion striking out 12."[6]

The second playoff game in the Little World Series again pitted Cashion against Asbury Park's best. As he had in all of the previous playoff games, my brother prevailed. "The new Shore champions won the game as early as the fourth inning, when they added two more runs and took a convincing 4–1 lead. With Dave (Dim) Cashion again in fine form, the Gulistans held the Asbury Park nine in check during the remainder of the fray and won going away by the score of 6–2, with Cashion permitting six hits and striking out ten batters."[7]

In early November, the entire Gulistans team was honored when the Foreman's Club of the Karagheusian rug mill held its annual dinner meeting at the American Hotel. The team received the trophy awarded to the Jersey Shore Baseball League Championship team.

As we have seen, my brother exhibited some exceptional skills during his peak years, mixed with bravado, which made him a very likable personality. "As opposing players tried to heckle the great Dave 'Dim' Cashion by waving handkerchiefs, Cashion retorted by pre-calling each pitch aloud and still managed to win game after game. Once, when his enemies goaded the red-faced hurler, Cashion looked down sternly at a young batter and prompted 'fastball, curveball, fastball,' and the hitter swung and missed all three pitches."[8]

Another of Cashion's amazing feats was the full pitching windup, in which his throwing arm would continue over his back and throw the pitch for a strike. Then there was the bat trick, where Cashion would toss the knob end of the bat against home plate, and the bat would bounce back into his waiting hands, ready to swing and, in turn, infuriate the opposing pitcher.

One of Dem's celebrated plays was a trick play to first base. With a runner on first base, he would intentionally throw the ball over the first baseman's head. The second baseman would position himself behind first base, catch the overthrown ball, and quickly throw to the shortstop covering second base for the easy tag out.

On April 5, 1948, a press release read, "Dave Cashion of Freehold, regarded as the best pitcher in the Jersey Shore Baseball league last year while performing with the Champion Freehold Gulistans, signed a contract to hurl for New Brunswick in the new Class B Colonial Baseball league . . . Before he entered the service in 1944, the Freehold pitcher, with the Salisbury, Md. Club in the Eastern Shore League, posted a 13–4 record.

"After returning from the Army, he joined the Freehold Gulistans in the Shore league and pitched them to the championship last year. Cashion will begin training Thursday afternoon at Ocean County Park, Lakewood. The New York Giants formerly used the diamond during the wartime ban on travel."[9]

Cashion's willingness to sign with the New Brunswick club could well have been inspired by his friendship with the player/manager Ed Kobesky. While Cashion was at Salisbury, Kobesky was the player/manager, playing third base and outfield and having several stints behind the plate. The franchise had been the New London Raiders the previous year.

They moved to New Brunswick for financial reasons, and by mid-1948 they had again relocated to Kingston, New York, and were called the Kingston Colonials. Kobesky had a

Dem with manager Ed Kobesky of New London in 1949. Courtesy of Cashion archives

great year in 1948, hitting twenty-one homers and winning the batting championship with an average of .396. Dem felt a kinship with Kobesky, as both had baseball in their blood.

"Kobesky had nothing but praise for Cashion after the big fellow completed his second day of work with the new team. 'Dave has more stuff now and better form. He has a better follow thru too, and seems headed for a good year.' For Cashion, it's almost a matter of whether he'll be able to get into the higher bracket of organized ball. For if he fails here, he'll be considered thru with plans of advancing a notch higher in baseball—and he'll throw aside hopes of more money. . . . But Kobesky has confidence in Cashion, pointing to the fact that he's a good runner, tho he is around the 30 year mark."[10] Interestingly, the official "Baseball Reference" for David E. Cashion lists his birth date as 1924, rather than the actual date of 1918, perhaps intentionally misleading.

Holding His Own

Early in his playing days with the Kingston nine, Cashion held his own in a competitive league. One reporter noted, "Dave Cashion, Freehold's only ball player in organized baseball today, is swinging a powerful bat and holding his own on the mound for the Kingston Colonials, formerly New Brunswick Hubs. . . . Cashion recently chalked up another mound victory, winning over Bridgeport. Along with his pitching performance, he contributed some heavy hitting, getting three doubles in four trips to the plate."[11]

Cashion went on to have a 4–6 pitching record and a batting average of .240, with one homer to his credit. Kobesky used Cashion in the outfield and at first base to help with the team's batting. During this season, my brother earned another sobriquet. He was called "Bobo" by his teammates, and we will never know why.[12]

While the club finished fourth in the league, the fans expressed their appreciation by collecting money for the players. The members of the 1948 team received $21.25 apiece as a result of the fans' contributions.[13] For a portion of the season, Kobesky was sidelined, and it is noteworthy that Cashion became the acting manager.

While Cashion was battling opposing teams in the Colonial League, the Freehold Gulistans had another banner year. Another hurling ace was leading the Gulistans toward first place in the Jersey Shore League. Ralph Steinberg was a high school pitching star. He had pitched two no-hitters and would have had a third if a single in the first inning hadn't marred that feat. His backstop in high school was Bobby Hayes, the brother of professional baseball catcher Frankie Hayes.

Cashion's Colonial League season ended in September, just in time for him to join the Gulistans as they entered the Shore Conference playoffs. On September 19, 1948, the Long Branch Green Sox met the Gulistans for a twin bill at the Lincoln Street field. In the opening game, Ralph Steinberg's pitching was subpar. While he only allowed two singles, he walked eleven, and the team was behind at the end of seven innings. However, the Gulistans managed to push over the winning runs in the eighth inning and win 5–3.

The second game was a different story. "Combining a 20-hit barrage . . . with the spectacular two-hit pitching of Dave Cashion . . . the Gulistans made a farce of the afternoon piece, scoring in all but the second canto of the abbreviated seven-inning struggle. . . . Cashion aided his cause with a double and a home run. The final tally was a 17–0 win for the Gulistans."[14]

After beating the West Belmar Blackhawks 4–0, the Gulistans faced the Red Bank Towners for the Shore Conference Championship. The two teams had previously met for the championship in 1946, and the Towners were victorious. This time, however, the Towners were facing the reigning champs.

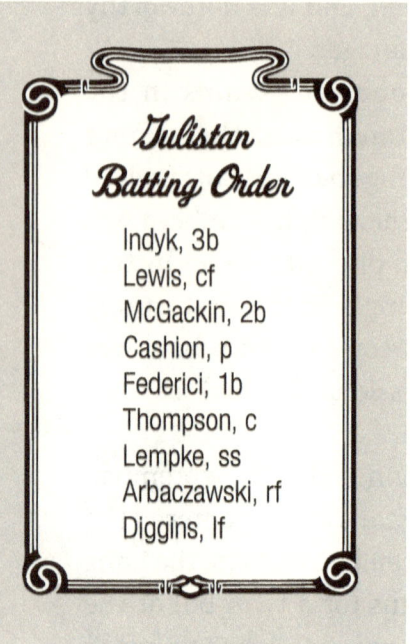

Gulistan Batting Order

Indyk, 3b
Lewis, cf
McGackin, 2b
Cashion, p
Federici, 1b
Thompson, c
Lempke, ss
Arbaczawski, rf
Diggins, lf

The two-out-of-three play-off started at the Red Bank diamond on October 3, 1948. "Big Dave 'Dim' Cashion collared the Red Bank hitters, allowing only six hits, all of them singles. The Gulistans squeezed by the Towners by the score of 3–2."[15]

The second game, played at the Lincoln Street field the following Sunday, did not favor the Gulistans. The Towners knocked in six runs off Ralph Steinberg. Cashion came in to relieve Ralph, but the Towners pushed across enough runs to win 8–7.

The league decided to hold the final decisive game for the Jersey Shore Baseball League Championship on the following Sunday, and, with a coin toss, Freehold's Lincoln Street field was the selected site.

For this pivotal game, Gene Briggs, the longtime Gulistan manager, went with his usual strong batting order, with Cashion in the cleanup slot.

The Gulistans were too much for the Towners in this contest. "The talented Gulistans won their second straight league championship by outscoring the Red Bank Towners 8–2. A crowd of about 900 saw the game. The Gulistans combined fancy six-hit pitching by the veteran Dave (Dim) Cashion and a solid 10-hit attack to pound out its decisive decision in the rubber engagement. Cashion was the complete master of his opposition. Cashion retired 12 straight batsmen from the third to the seventh frame. The speedy curveball artist registered ten strikeouts and had almost perfect control, giving up only one pass. In addition to chucking a brilliant game, he collected a double and two singles to share batting honors with Joe Indyk."[16]

As a local Freehold sportswriter opined, "For the top thrill of 1948, some might point out the inspirational (and perspirational) dynamo of David Cashion. The irrepressible David took up the lethargic Gulistans about playoff time and soared them into the title. He mowed down the opposition with remarkable ease and rattled the fences with valuable base hits when they were needed. All this after a stint with Kingston, NY Class B baseball, where as an alternate first baseman and pitcher, he slugged .309 and won well over half of his decisions as a twirler."[17]

Despite the 1948 championship, the 1949 season didn't go so well for the Gulistans. They finished in seventh place in the Jersey Shore League with a 9–9 record. However, there were some bright spots. Steinberg continued to be on fire and pitched a sparkling game against Keansburg A.C. on August 8, 1949. Only a single in the ninth inning marred his bid for a no-hitter, along with fifteen strikeouts. The final tally was 14–0.

On September 4, 1949, Cashion kept the team's thin hopes for a playoff berth alive with a 19–1 win over Freehold A.C. The opposing pitcher was Gene Briggs, former manager of the Gulistans.

The team's final chance for a playoff berth came on September 11, 1946. Gil Toon, Gulistans pitcher, kept the Red Bank Rangers under control until the seventh inning, when Red Bank went ahead 3–2. The Gulistans managed to tie the game in the eighth inning. In the tenth inning, Cashion smashed a towering home run over the left-field fence at the

Newman Springs field, putting the Gulistans out front. The Rangers tied the score in the bottom of the tenth. Cashion was brought in to relieve Toon, and the Rangers managed to squeak out the win in the bottom of the eleventh, eliminating the Gulistans from the playoffs.[18]

While Cashion was playing for the Gulistans, he also spent some time playing with the Brooklyn Bushwicks. His old friend from the Belmar Braves, Paul Schreiber, had spent some time with the team, and it is possible that he provided my brother's intro there.

The Bushwicks were an independent semiprofessional team that played games almost totally in Dexter Park in Queens from 1913 to 1951. They were unique at the time for fielding multiethnic rosters. They played what amounted to exhibition games against barnstorming Negro League teams, minor league baseball teams, and other semipro teams. Many of the famous players of the time came to play exhibitions at Dexter Park, including Dizzy Dean, Hank Greenberg, Joe DiMaggio, Babe Ruth, Lou Gehrig, and Joe Medwick.[19]

Giving Back to the Game

At this point, Cashion's pitching arm was starting to show its age, and he wasn't throwing the whistling fastball as frequently. He had his curveball and knuckleball, and he would continue to pitch as needed into the 1960s. However, his batting eye never left him.

In May 1950, in a Gulistan game against Whitesville, "Dave Cashion won the tilt in the last licks with his third round-tripper in as many tilts, a tremendous blast over the left-center field barricades at Lincoln Street field."[20] The lead sportswriter for the *Asbury Park Press* wrote, "Dave

Cashion of the Freehold Gulistans has established a record in the Jersey Shore Baseball league that will probably never be broken. Dave has hit home runs in each of the three games the Gulistans have played."[21]

Another example of Cashion's all-around baseball skill was evident in September of 1950. In a game against the West Belmar Blackhawks, Cashion donned the "tools of ignorance." "Dem played the entire game at catcher and, after letting two pitches by him in the first, played steady ball at the unfamiliar position. He called balls and strikes louder—if not as accurately—than the umpire."[22]

The Gulistans finished the 1950 season tied for second place, with a 12–6 record. "Dem's batting average for the year was .311, as cleanup man, four of them round-trippers."[23]

As noted earlier, Dem's father was, for many years, Freehold's outstanding catcher. That was the opinion of Mayor Fred Quinn, himself the borough's top pitcher for much of the same period. Along came Dem's son to shine in the baseball spotlight.

However, more Cashion ball players were coming along—Dem's sons, Don and Wayne, and me (his little brother). "In July 1951, Don, age 11, pitched two consecutive no-hitters with the St. Rose of Lima Little League team against Englishtown. Don hurled both no-hitters four days apart, winning the first 9–2 and the second 6–1. He fanned a total of 23 and walked nine in the two six-inning games. Englishtown was the victim both times."[24]

While Don was starring with the St. Rose of Lima Little League team, I, as a ten-year-old, did not even try out for the team. I had no confidence in my baseball playing. I needed a lot of coaching to gain the confidence to play in organized ball. Fortunately, my brother Dem, home from his minor league days, was available to devote time to teach me the fundamentals of the game.

Although Dem started me on the road to pitching, he quickly turned me into a catcher. I spent countless hours with him learning how to catch and hit in the backyard of 27 McLean Street, and when the next St. Rose of Lima baseball season rolled around, I was the team's starting catcher and heavy hitter. Dem would become the manager/coach of the St. Rose of Lima team and would instill in me the baseball drive that carried me throughout my future playing days.

Dem's youngest son, Wayne, would also develop into an excellent ball player. Starting at second base with St. Rose of Lima, Wayne moved over to the Freehold Little League. In 1955, he mowed down fifteen on strikeouts in one game and made the Little League All-Star team.

Wayne had an ERA of 0.84 and was named best Babe Ruth pitcher in 1957. In 1958, the opening day of Babe Ruth League, Wayne pitched a sparkling two-hitter with seventeen strikeouts. The peak of his pitching career came on May 26, 1958, when he threw a no-hitter with fourteen strikeouts, making him the third member of the Cashion family to toss a no-hitter.[25]

During this period, ball playing remained a significant role in Dem's life. But this is also the time when he started on his journey of managing and coaching and, in so doing, helped hundreds of young men reach their potential on the diamond. Dem was also constantly seeking to promote baseball in Freehold and throughout Monmouth County.

In addition to his stint as manager/coach of the St. Rose of Lima team in 1951, the Farm Belt League officials named

Dem as chairman of the league. That same year, he managed the nascent Freehold Merchant team and was a significant player in the start of Little Bigger League baseball.

The Little Bigger League provided a baseball league for players between Little League and high school, playing initially at the Freehold High School field. Cashion managed one of the first teams in the league while also taking charge of enhancing the Lincoln Street field for play the following year.

In 1953, the league was named the Freehold Babe Ruth League, and play commenced on the newly acquired Nescafé field in 1954. Cashion would guide hundreds of young players in the Babe Ruth League as manager of teams during 1952 and from 1958 to 1962, and then with my assistance as a coach from 1959 to 1961.[26]

Sensing a baseball void for alumni of the Babe Ruth League, Cashion convinced the American Legion and the Cameron-Roberson Agency to sponsor a team. From 1955 to 1957, Cashion managed and coached an imposing Legion team, playing games throughout the Central Jersey area. Among the top players on this team were outstanding pitchers Ed Ostrowski and John McCarthy.

One of the American Legion season highlights was an All-Star game played at Fort Monmouth. The baseball commissioner of the Legion League was "Mule" Hass, a former player with the Phillies and athletic director at Fort Monmouth. Cashion knew Mule through his major league scouting contacts. Interestingly, Dem's wife Betty once remarked that the first time she saw a World Series ring was when she met Mule, who had played on World Series championship teams with the Phillies in 1929 and 1930.[27]

Good Fundraiser Too

In 1951, Cashion established the Freehold Merchants and acted as player-manager of the club. He had an uncanny ability to gain backers for his clubs over the years. "He gained the support of the local chamber of commerce, and Ed Bachman, Assistant Manager of the rug mill, granted the use of the Gulistans' equipment. Wynn's Jewelry Store would give a trophy to the Freehold player with the top batting average. Sid's Men's Shop offered $5 credit for a shutout, and home runs will each earn $1 credit. Al's Bootery offered a pair of 'Florsheim' men's shoes for bases-loaded homers."[28]

By the end of the first season, Cashion managed to pull off one more amazing promotional feat. He secured a working agreement with the Philadelphia Phillies. The Phillies supplied uniforms and equipment for the following year in return for first choice on promising Freehold baseball players.[29]

During the stretch of Freehold Merchant seasons, from 1951 to 1953, several outstanding players worked and played with Cashion. Guggy Lewis, known for his days as the star center fielder of the Gulistans, and Dick Skehan assisted as coaches. In July 1951, Ralph Steinberg was on the mound and pitched a one-hitter with nineteen strikeouts. His battery mate was Cashion, once again demonstrating his versatility. Cashion had three hits that afternoon, including two home runs.

On the few rare occasions when he would escape the diamond, Cashion participated in local church minstrel shows at St. Rose of Lima. He had a decent voice and enjoyed participating in singing groups. One of his performances was at the March 1954 minstrel. The packed hall listened to Cashion, Paul Fitch, Gene Briggs, and Claude Cornell dazzle the audience with their renditions of "I See the Moon" and "Heart of My Heart."[30]

An inquiring reporter once asked Cashion how long he would remain in the league. He answered, "When the kids,

The Cashion boys from 1958 (left to right): my brother "Dem," yours truly, and Dem's sons, Don and Wayne. Courtesy of Cashion archives

Don and Wayne, start playing in the league, that's when I'll retire."[31] The next team that Cashion created, the Freehold Townsmen (1958–1964), saw his son Don, his brother Glenn, and, briefly, his son Wayne playing beside him.

The Freehold Transcript ran a lovely photo of the "Cashion Clan" in August of 1958, featuring Dem, Glenn, Don, and Wayne holding baseballs. The good news is that Dem did not stop playing ball. His DNA wouldn't allow him to avoid the baseball fields.

The Townsmen were very competitive in the Jersey Shore League, although they never came out on top. McCarthy and Ostrowski were the pitching aces in the early years. McCarthy and Don Cashion and, of course, Dem were the key pitchers in the club's later years. Sid Blacknall, who played a lot of ball with the Negro League, also brought strength to the pitching roster.

Age was starting to take its toll on Dem, as this 1958 story demonstrates: "Dave put himself into the Townsmen game against the Norwoods and somehow reached first base. The next batter, Tommy DiSalvo, sacrificed, and the pitcher, VanDyke, threw the ball to second in an attempt to force Cashion . . . Fortunately for the Townsmen but unfortunately for Dim, the ball went wild into centerfield and Cashion, completely exhausted from sliding into second base, was expected to get up and run. All pooped out, but still game, Dim chugged and churned around third and let go full steam for home plate. He hit the dirt, was called safe by the umpire, but old Dim just couldn't get up enough energy to get off his back for almost a full minute."[32]

While he undoubtedly had slowed down, Cashion remained a formidable batter. On July 3, 1960, at Manasquan's home field, the Townsmen trounced Manasquan 14–3. The hitting barrage included three hits by Glenn Cashion, a three-run home run by Roger Kane, and Dem's prodigious, sky-high homer, hitting the house in left field.

The 1961 season ended with Roger Kane leading in batting with a .371 average and Dem right behind him with a .303 average. The team had to cease playing when financial backing was not available.

By 1963, the number of spectators at the Institute Streetfield was sparse. The caliber of the baseball action with the Legion team, the Freehold Merchants, and the Freehold Townsmen was excellent. However, television and other leisurely pursuits kept the fans away. The smaller crowds did not deter Cashion. He kept injecting new life into Freehold baseball by starting new teams.

Cashion next teamed up with Abe Steinberg, a local businessman, to apply for admittance of a Freehold team into the Ed Carleton Baseball League in 1963.[33] This team was composed of boys in the sixteen-to-eighteen-year-old age group. It operated for several seasons.

Cashion's last team was the Freehold entry into the Ed Carleton League in 1971. He was instrumental in convincing the Jersey Shore League to allow Freehold to enter a new team. As usual, Cashion "was able to reach out to top-notch players from the area to join the new Freehold club, e.g., Matawan's Larry Shaw, a combination pitcher-outfielder-first baseman, who the Minnesota Twins had recently released."[34]

Even at this stage in his career, Cashion could not remain seated on the bench. In July 1973, "Dem put the Freehold ahead on a line drive, over the shortstop, two-run single in the fourth inning, and they went on to win the game 11–9."[35]

Bring on the Old-Timers

Cashion loved to organize and play in "old-timers" games. Perhaps the first one he managed was in 1952 at the Lincoln Street field. The "Stars of Yesterday," a collection of good players from Freehold and the vicinity, were matched against the New Jersey Colored All-Stars in a benefit game for Ed Lempke, an injured Freehold ball player.

Appearing at the benefit was the entire championship Gulistan team of 1947–48. A local favorite, Babe Cawley, sang "'The Star-Spangled Banner.' Among the players from yesterday were Scotty Carswell, Bill Rhoades, Oodles Vanderveer, 'Nipper' Madge, Tucker Potter, 'Shorty' Taylor, Ed King, Art Marvel, O. Kehs, H. Schanck, Sam McGackin, Dave McCollory, John Tilton, Joe McGlory, Dave Thompson, Bill Tela, 'Gibby' Toon, John Farmer, Marty Diggins, Dante Federici, Guggy Lewis, and Harold Daley."[36]

Cashion also orchestrated other "old-timers" games throughout the 1950s; many of these would feature local and county politicians, bands, parades through town, and refreshments at the Legion following the games.

In 1957, Cashion doggedly managed to corral 135 players to participate in a game at the Freehold Regional athletic field. During the 1960s, Cashion participated in numerous old-timers games throughout the Jersey Shore. He was always the starting pitcher and managed to get a few hits.

With Cashion's professional league contacts and his ability to recognize baseball talent, he was a "bird dog" scout for major league baseball for a few decades. Cashion and longtime Phillies scout Jocko Collins were good friends, and Cashion constantly referred ball players with major league potential to Collins.

"In 1958, Dem took John McCarthy, Roger Kane, and Bruce Phillips to Phillipsburg for a Philadelphia tryout."[37] "In 1959, Dem organized a tryout camp with the Washington Senators in Freehold."[38] "In 1965 Dem assisted in running a multi-major league team tryout camp in Jamesburg, NJ."[39]

When Cashion wasn't on the field playing ball, he was there as an umpire. Just as his father had transitioned to umpiring after his days as a catcher, Cashion loved to don the blue shirt and umpire at Babe Ruth, Ed Carleton, high school, and Jersey Shore games. He was active as an umpire for about thirty years as a Jersey Shore Umpires Association member and with the New Jersey State Federation of Umpires.

Cashion was a visionary for Monmouth County baseball in many ways, including the old-timers games. "He was a proponent for the erection of a centrally located sports stadium to provide sorely needed facilities for those athletically inclined and for those who like to watch sports."[40]

Sadly, Cashion's vision of a countywide sports stadium never materialized. As his final days approached, he often reached out to the local news media and made guest appearances on the local Asbury Park radio station. "He had hoped to start a Shore Baseball Hall of Fame and was planning to hold an organization meeting in the near future."[41]

Following several months of ill health, Cashion died of congestive heart failure on the afternoon of April 5, 1975, at the age of fifty-five.

Singing His Praises

"Baseball will always remember Dave. When you think about baseball in Freehold, you've got to think about Dave."

—CHARLIE "MALKO" MALEKOVICH, *former teammate and Babe Ruth manager*[42]

"He had a heart like a hotel. There was room for everybody."

—BOB GEIGER, *Keyport police chief and former teammate*[43]

"I've seen a lot of coaches around Freehold, or at least a lot of people who call themselves coaches, but I don't think they knew the game like Dim did."

—ED LEMPKE, *former teammate*[44]

"I remember that game a couple of years ago. It was one of the hottest days of the year. Dem got up there, and there was a bunch of people sitting under the trees, and somebody said, 'Who's that fat old man?' I said, 'Watch, you'll see,' and boy, he jumped on it."

—TOM BRERETON, *former teammate and manager of Ed Carleton League*[45]

"*I remember playing against him. I was a fastball pitcher out of high school, and when I saw this big man walk up to the plate, I said to myself, 'Ah, watch me throw this ball right by him.' The next thing I knew, the ball was hit by me.*"

—FRANK HAVILAND, *former player and officer of Jersey Shore League*[46]

"*Dim probably taught me more about baseball than all of my other coaches combined. He knew more about baseball than any man around here.*"

—ROGER KANE, *former teammate and former Mayor of Freehold*[47]

"*Dem was my idol. I tried to model myself after him. When I watched him play at Lincoln Street, he inspired me. He was full of humor, a fantastic athlete and just a wonderful human being.*"[48]

—RALPH STEINBERG, *former star pitcher for the Gulistans and the Merchants*

"*I think that I never met anyone who loved baseball more than he did. You could just feel the connection he had to the game by watching him move around the ball field as a coach or just talking to him. He's the only person I met in years of involvement in baseball that I think of when I hear the phrase 'Old School.' I think of him often and always very fondly.*"[49]

—BARRY DRUESNE, *former player with Dem's last managed team, the County Seaters*

EPILOGUE: THE LITTLE BROTHER WEIGHS IN

When asked by the Freehold Transcript *reporter for comments* on the death of my brother, I said, "He was the father of baseball to hundreds of kids. He lived the life he wanted to lead, and that life was baseball."[50]

These chapters depict the rich baseball life Dem led. Dem's car was always full of baseball paraphernalia. He probably drove more ball players in his car than members of his own family. He wore out the black rotary dial telephone at our mother's home talking to players, coaches, old-timers, scouts, business owners, and the media.

Dem, however, was an enigma. During his life, he fought the demons that plagued him. There were times of depression and silence, and there were times of exuberance. His bipolar personality affected his life and his baseball experiences. When he was "himself," he was the warmest soul you would ever meet. He could charm you and convince you that your contribution to the baseball future of Freehold was in your best interest.

His teammates and managers held Dem in high esteem for his baseball skills and leadership, during his time in the minor leagues and at the Jersey Shore League. One sportswriter, who was a classmate of Dem's at Red Bank Catholic High School, recalled how their freshman class, after an acquaintance of only a few hours, elected him class president by a heavy vote.[51]

Red Pierson, who was president of the Jersey Shore Baseball League for many years, remembered Dem very well from their playing days and instituted four annual awards, one of which was for the best pitcher in the league. He named it the "Dave Cashion Award."

I and other members of my family witnessed Dem at his low points and felt helpless. He did undergo some treatment early on; however, his condition was generally left to "time out" until he reached the high points again. This way of living resulted in low job stability and impacted what could have been even more remarkable baseball accomplishments.

But what he did accomplish in his short time on this earth was enormous, as bespeak the hundreds of newspaper articles proclaiming his baseball prowess and desire to spread the "baseball gospel" throughout Freehold and Monmouth counties. Dem was one of a kind, and he was indeed loved by all who knew him.

Dem, "Mr. Baseball of Freehold," you will never be forgotten by your family and your many baseball friends.

APPENDIX 1

The "Tools of Ignorance"

Many of you are familiar with the stellar career of Gary Carter (Montreal Expos, New York Mets), who was inducted into the Baseball Hall of Fame in Cooperstown in 2003. As I pondered that accomplishment, I couldn't help but relive my baseball life and reflect on the evolution of the catcher position over the life span of baseball. Carter is the fourteenth catcher to be elected to the Hall of Fame, and he and the others embody the toughness and skill necessary for that position.

Yes, I too was a catcher. I caught for seventeen years, from 1950 to 1967. My teams included the following:

- Saint Rose of Lima Little League in Freehold;
- Red Sox in the Freehold Babe Ruth League;
- Freehold High School;
- Brown University;
- Freehold Townsmen in the Jersey Shore Baseball League; and
- several softball teams, including the NJ State Champion Freehold Jaycees.

Over the years, we won some championships, and I held my own in that baseball arena; however, the skill set possessed by a major league catcher, let alone a Hall of Famer, far exceeded my performance during my gallant catching years.

A catcher is the team's cornerstone (pardon my bias), and I was fortunate that I never had a coach call the pitches during my entire seventeen years. I was the quarterback of the baseball diamond and involved in every pitch.

I recently attended a college reunion where a fraternity brother, whom I hadn't seen in twenty-five years, turned to me and said, "I never realized how stupid you were." Refraining from a more drastic pugilistic move, I said, "Mike, what do you mean?" His reply was not what I expected. He said, "Well, when you were catching in college, I just thought that you were stupid to play that position, with all of that silly equipment, that is, the 'tools of ignorance.'"

He added, "Now that I better understand the game, I have come to appreciate catchers and feel that they are the brains behind the team." Rest assured, yours truly breathed a sigh of relief. My mental capacity was not really in question. He had given me a most welcome compliment.

But what about those tools of ignorance? What is the history behind the phrase? Clearly, as in all of baseball, there has to be an evolution of the catching position. In the 1860s, the catcher was called the "behind" and he, along with the rest of the team, did not wear gloves. "The catcher played directly behind the bat only when runners were on the bases, and later after two strikes on the batter. Catchers were the first to require a glove."[1]

"One of the first to don a catcher's mask was James Alexander Tyng of Harvard in 1875. The donning of the mask was met with nineteenth-century raspberries; however, eventually, all catchers donned the mask." "In 1884, Jack Clemens of Keystone club wore the first chest protector, and he also took many fans and player criticism." [2]

In 1893, modern baseball began; it was that year that the pitching distance was increased from fifty-five feet to sixty feet six inches. This was the last radical change in the game's evolution. That same year there was an attempt to move the bases to ninety-three feet, from ninety feet, but that move failed. The bases remain at the same distance established by the National Association of Base Ball Players in 1857. The last adornment to the "tools of ignorance" was the shin guard.

"Roger Bresnahan of the NY Giants in 1907 donned the shin guard and this time there was no negative reaction. Receivers were tired of the battering their legs received from crazily breaking spitters and other trick deliveries, as well as 'flying spikes.'"[3]

The family consisting of the mask, the chest protector, and the shin guards make up the well-respected tools of ignorance. "This armor kit was lovingly dubbed 'tools of ignorance' by Harold 'Muddy' Ruel, a backstop and a lawyer who caught for greats like Walter Johnson with the Washington Nationals in the 1920s."[4] We who have been there can significantly appreciate them; while I may have some sore knees and crooked fingers, the tools of ignorance kept me safe for those seventeen years.

May all the catchers out there join me in congratulating Gary Carter. To some degree, we know what it means to say "I was a catcher."

APPENDIX 2

Thoughts on the Ban on Home Plate Collisions

Most of you know that Major League Baseball adopted a rule in 2014 to effectively ban home plate collisions. The rule reads as follows:

The base runner is not allowed to deviate from his direct path to initiate contact with the catcher (or any player covering the plate). Runners are considered to be in violation of this rule if they collide with the catcher in cases where a slide could have been used to avoid the collision.

This rule is still in effect today.

I first donned the tools of ignorance in 1950 as a player for St. Rose of Lima, a team in the Farm Belt League, a precursor to the Freehold Little League. For the next eighteen years, inning by inning, I caught for a wide variety of teams, ultimately retiring around 1968.

In my early days of catching, my size was a distinct advantage. My early nickname of "Moose" may explain why few attempts to "take me out" at home plate were successful. The base runner was usually the one who left the collision in a daze.

Early on, thanks to the professional tutelage of my brother, I learned the mechanics of blocking home plate. While I can't recall the exact date of my first collision at home plate, it had to be in the early days of my St. Rose of Lima experience. For many years, my bulk protected me from the home plate clashes. However, it only took a few years until the other players were equal or greater in size.

How many "major" home plate collisions did I experience during my career? I don't know for sure. However, I clearly remember about a dozen episodes; I know there were many more that I have blocked out of my memory. The memorable collisions fall into two categories: pure delight as I lifted the player over my shoulder, and pain and grogginess immediately after the collision.

There were several collisions where the over-six-foot player thought he would barrel into me, with no slide, and knock me over. Any good catcher loves that situation because if the catcher knows the mechanics of the trade, he will lower his body, hit the runner in the midsection with his shoulder, and raise the player over his head. The runner will generally do a nice somersault and land behind the catcher, not only to be declared out, but ending up in a most embarrassing position.

The other type of collision would see me going into a kneeling position, guarding the plate, and the runner would accelerate and attempt to get me to drop the ball by using either a shoulder crash or a hard slide. While I don't recall ever dropping the ball, I certainly remember the effects on my body.

However, I was young and invincible, and I just brushed it off and went about my catching duties. I'm very fortunate that my body didn't suffer from those incidents. My knees are still original, and I was able to run five marathons in the '70s and '80s.

When MLB was contemplating banning home plate collisions, I had mixed emotions. Pete Rose stated his objections, and I am sure other traditionalists felt that such a ruling would weaken the game. For the most part, I am a traditionalist; however, when I look at the multiple MLB home plate collisions over the past few decades, I see that many are indeed brutal.

The sport of baseball has survived since the late nineteenth century, and it has undergone numerous rule changes. As this book attests, I come from a baseball family. My family has played baseball since the late 1880s in the Freehold area.

As a catcher, I enjoyed watching other catchers' skill at the moment of the home plate collision. However, the health of players, both runner and catcher, is more important than the thrill of the collision. I still have memories of those collisions, and that will suffice; I don't have to relive them while watching an MLB game.

APPENDIX 3

Dem's All-Time Freehold Baseball Team

Who better to pick a Freehold all-time baseball team than "Mr. Baseball of Freehold," Dave "Dem" Cashion? My brother watched many great ball players and played with and against many of Freehold's finest players, from the late 1920s through the mid-1970s.

In the spring of 1958, the *Freehold Transcript* asked Dem to come up with his dream team as part of an article they were working on. Here are Dem's selections.

Pitchers
Cecil Splitter
Harry Petty
Cooney Haberman
Fred Quinn
Eddie King
Charlie Lugannani
Gibby Toon (the only southpaw)
Bill Tela

Catchers
Henny Dane
Frank Hayes

First basemen
Oodles Vanderveer
Dante Federici

Second basemen
Ike Wooley
Sam McGackin

Third basemen
Chubby Perrine
Myron VanCleaf

Shortstops	Center fielders
Art Manuel	Billy Rhoades
Irish Hyres	Dave Egbert

Left fielders	Right fielders
Gene Williams	Tucker Potter
Walt Briggs	"Farmer John" Arbaczawski

Managers

E. I. Vanderveer, who managed numerous championship clubs

Gene Briggs, who managed the Gulistans to the championships

Other fine managers were Joe Crotchfelt, Freehold Firemen; Doc Wood, Colonials; J. Percy Anderson, Holy Name; Charlie "Malko" Malekovich, Trylons and Freehold A.C.; William Bellamy, Cubs.

As a *Freehold Transcript* reporter rightly concluded, "There was only one thing missing in his All-Star team. He had picked eight pitchers and two first basemen. But what would the Freehold All-Stars be without Dave 'Dem' Cashion?"

ENDNOTES

Chapter 1: Baseball Beginnings

1. Geoffrey C. Ward and Ken Burns, *Baseball: An Illustrated History* (New York: Alfred A. Knopf, 1994), 3.
2. John Zinn, *A Cradle of the National Pastime: New Jersey Baseball 1855-1880* (Princeton, New Jersey: Morven Museum and Garden, 2019), 11–13.
3. Geoffrey C. Ward and Ken Burns, *Baseball: An Illustrated History* (New York: Alfred A. Knopf, 1994), 3.
4. John Montgomery Ward, *Base-Ball: How to Become a Player* (Philadelphia: The Athletic Publishing Company, 1888), 12–13.
5. Geoffrey C. Ward and Ken Burns, *Baseball: An Illustrated History* (New York: Alfred A. Knopf, 1994), 4.
6. Harold Peterson, "Baseball's Johnny Appleseed" in *The Baseball Book* (New York: Sports Illustrated Books, 2008), 46.
7. Ibid.
8. Henry Chadwick, *Base-Ball Player: A Compendium of the Game* (New York: Irwin P. Beadle & Company, 1860), 2.
9. Geoffrey C. Ward and Ken Burns, *Baseball: An Illustrated History* (New York: Alfred A. Knopf, 1994), 6.
10. Ibid., pp. 7–8.

11. John Montgomery Ward, *Base-Ball: How to Become a Player* (Philadelphia: The Athletic Publishing Company, 1888), Foreword.

12. John Zinn, *A Cradle of the National Pastime: New Jersey Baseball 1855–1880* (Princeton, New Jersey: Morven Museum and Garden, 2019), 21, 29.

Chapter 2: 1857–1900: Freehold Embraces Baseball

1. *Monmouth Inquirer*, May 23, 1857

2. *Monmouth Democrat*, June 15, 1858

3. George B. Kirsch, *Baseball in Blue and Gray: The National Pastime During the Civil War* (Princeton, New Jersey: Princeton University Press, 2003), 47.

4. *Monmouth Democrat*, September 14, 1865

5. *Monmouth Democrat*, July 26, 1860

6. *Monmouth Democrat*, November 30, 1865

7. *Monmouth Democrat*, May 29, 1866

8. *New York Times*, June 9, 1874

9. *Monmouth Democrat*, August 8, 1867

10. *Monmouth Democrat*, August 22, 1867

11. *Monmouth Democrat*, May 9, 1872

12. *Monmouth Democrat*, June 6, 1872

13. *Monmouth Democrat*, June 13, 1872

14. *Monmouth Democrat*, October 10, 1872

15. *Monmouth Democrat*, September 19, 1872; October 10, 1872

16. *Monmouth Democrat*, October 12, 1876

17. United States Department of the Interior

18. *Monmouth Inquirer*, July 23, 1874

19. *Monmouth Inquirer*, April 23, 1874

20. *Monmouth Democrat*, October 1, 1886

21. *Monmouth Inquirer*, June 10, 1886

22. *Monmouth Inquirer*, July 5, 1887

23. *Monmouth Democrat*, July 21, 1887

24. *Monmouth Democrat*, August 18, 1887

25. *Monmouth Democrat*, September 22, 1887

26. *Monmouth Democrat*, July 26, 1888

27. *Monmouth Democrat*, May 22, 1891

28. *Monmouth Democrat*, June 11, 1891; July 9, 1891

29. *Monmouth Democrat*, May 28, 1871

30. *Monmouth Democrat*, July 2, 1891

31. *Monmouth Democrat*, July 9, 1891

32. Ibid.

33. *Monmouth Democrat*, July 30, 1891

34. *Monmouth Democrat*, August 6, 1891

35. *Monmouth Democrat*, July 30, 1891

36. *Monmouth Democrat*, August 11, 1891

37. *Monmouth Democrat*, August 20, 1891

38. *Monmouth Democrat*, September 3, 1891

39. *Monmouth Democrat*, March 17, 1892

40. *Monmouth Democrat*, July 7, 1892

41. *Monmouth Democrat*, April 27, 1893

42. *Freehold Transcript*, June 18, 1897

43. *Monmouth Democrat*, June 30, 1893

44. *Freehold Transcript*, July 28, 1893

45. *Monmouth Democrat*, July 28, 1893

46. *Monmouth Democrat*, June 16, 1893

47. *Monmouth Democrat*, April 26, 1900

48. *Freehold Transcript*, July 22, 1898; August 5, 1898

Chapter 3: 1900–1916: Baseball Takes Off in Freehold

1. *Monmouth Democrat*, August 2, 1901

2. *Monmouth Democrat*, May 16, 1901

3. *Monmouth Democrat*, June 27, 1901

4. *Monmouth Democrat*, June 13, 1901

5. *Monmouth Democrat*, July 11, 1901; July 18, 1901
6. *Monmouth Inquirer*, May 16, 1902
7. *Freehold Transcript*, May 1, 1958
8. *Monmouth Democrat*, August 4, 1904
9. *Monmouth Democrat*, August 10, September 7, October 19, 1905
10. *Freehold Transcript*, September 29, 1944
11. *Monmouth Democrat*, May 9, 1907
12. *Monmouth Democrat*, August 3, 1933
13. *Freehold Transcript*, May 10, 1912
14. Ibid.
15. *Monmouth Democrat*, August 1, 1940
16. *Daily Record*, Long Branch, August 23, 1922
17. *Monmouth Democrat*, August 1, 1905
18. *Freehold Transcript*, May 2, 1913
19. *Monmouth Democrat*, May 11, 1905
20. *100 Years–Our Hometown*, Borough of Freehold (booklet), 32.
21. *Monmouth Democrat*, September 15, 1904
22. *Monmouth Democrat*, June 1, 1904
23. *Monmouth Democrat*, April 6, 1905
24. *Freehold Transcript*, September 15, 1905
25. *Asbury Park Press*, October 9, 1905
26. *Freehold Transcript*, September 15, 1905
27. Negro League Baseball Players' Accounts: https://www.blackpast.org/african-american-history/philadelphia-giants-1902-1911/
28. *Asbury Park Press*, April 6, 1926
29. *Freehold Transcript*, April 2, 1964
30. *Monmouth Democrat*, July 8, 1920
31. *Asbury Park Press*, July 20, 1941
32. *Monmouth Democrat*, July 21, 1921
33. *Monmouth Democrat*, August 29, 1922

34. *Monmouth Democrat*, April 15, 1923

35. *Asbury Park Press*, July 2, 1923

36. *Asbury Park Press*, October 5, 1926

37. New York Times, October 12, 1926

38. *Asbury Park Press*, October 12, 1926

39. *Monmouth Democrat*, April 21, 1938

40. *Monmouth Inquirer*, July 10, 1884

41. *Monmouth Inquirer*, April 11, 1889

42. *Freehold Transcript*, October 16, 1908

43. *Asbury Park Press*, June 16, 1921

44. *Freehold Transcript*, August 11, 1944

45. *Monmouth Inquirer*, March 8, 1906; March 15, 1906;
    February 14, 1906

46. *Monmouth Democrat*, August 16, 1906

47. *Monmouth Democrat*, July 29, 1909

48. *Monmouth Democrat*, August 12, 1909

Chapter 4: 1916–1937: Record-Breaking Crowds

1. *Monmouth Democrat*, July 8, 1920

2. *Monmouth Democrat*, October 23, 1920

3. *Asbury Park Press*, July 20, 1921

4. *Monmouth Democrat*, November 9, 1922

5. *Monmouth Democrat*, June 28, 1923

6. *Asbury Park Press*, July 2, 1923

7. *Asbury Park Press*, December 1, 1923

8. *Monmouth Democrat*, January 3, 1924

9. *Monmouth Inquirer*, May 23, 1924

10. *Monmouth Democrat*, May 15, 1924

11. *Freehold Transcript*, September 22, 1916

12. *Asbury Park Press*, July 7, 1917

13. *Freehold Transcript*, July 13, 1917

14. *Monmouth Democrat*, June 5, 1919

15. *Freehold Transcript*, June 29, 1928

16. *Monmouth Democrat*, October 14, 1939

17. *Monmouth Democrat*, November 19, 1925

18. *Freehold Transcript*, September 16, 1932

19. *Freehold Transcript*, April 21, 1933; September 29, 1933

20. *Asbury Park Press*, October 16, 1933

21. *Asbury Park Press*, October 29, 1934

22. *Monmouth Democrat*, October 19, 1929; October 15, 1925

23. *Freehold Transcript*, April 19, 1929

24. *Monmouth Inquirer*, September 2, 1926

25. *Monmouth Inquirer*, May 23, 1931

26. *Freehold Transcript*, June 19, 1952

27. *Asbury Park Press*, August 14, 1925

28. *Freehold Transcript*, April 24, 1925

29. *Monmouth Inquirer*, July 9, 1925

30. *Monmouth Inquirer*, September 30, 1926

31. *Freehold Transcript*, May 15, 1925; February 10, 1928; *Monmouth, Democrat*, January 13, 1927

32. *Monmouth Inquirer*, July 26, 1923

33. *Monmouth Democrat*, August 14, 1924

34. *Monmouth Democrat*, June 16, 1927

35. *Monmouth Democrat*, July 31, 1930

36. *Monmouth Democrat*, February 2, 1933

37. *Monmouth Democrat*, August 23, 1934

38. *Monmouth Democrat*, October 11, 1934

39. *Monmouth Democrat*, September 12, 1935

40. *Monmouth Democrat*, November 7, 1935

41. *Monmouth Democrat*, October 24, 1935

42. *Freehold Transcript*, August 16, 1960

43. *Monmouth Democrat*, August 6, 1936

44. *Monmouth Democrat*, October 1, 1936

45. *Monmouth Democrat*, February 11, 1937

46. *Monmouth Democrat*, May 13, 1937
47. *Freehold Transcript*, June 15, 1928
48. *Monmouth Democrat*, June 21, 1934
49. *Freehold Transcript*, June 15, 1928 *Monmouth Democrat*, May 19, 1933
50. *Monmouth Democrat*, August 29, 1935
51. *Monmouth Democrat*, October 10, 1935
52. *Monmouth Democrat*, May 7, 1936
53. *Monmouth Democrat*, April 9, 1936; September 3, 1936
54. *Monmouth Democrat*, July 1, 1937
55. *Freehold Transcript*, October 25, 1935
56. *Morning Call*, Paterson, New Jersey, November 19, 1934
57. Nicholas Dawidoff, *The Catcher Was a Spy* (New York: Vintage Books, 1995), 94–95.
58. Louis Kaufman, Barbara Fitzgerald, and Tom Sewell, *Moe Berg: Athlete Scholar* (Boston: Little, Brown, 1974), 28.
59. Monmouth Democrat, June 25, 1936
60. Ibid.
61. *Freehold Transcript*, July 30, 1937

Chapter 5: 1937–1973: Fierce Competition

1. *Monmouth Democrat*, March 10, 1938; April 21, 1938
2. *Monmouth Democrat*, July 28, 1938
3. *Monmouth Democrat*, May 12, 1938
4. *Monmouth Democrat*, June 22, 1939
5. *Freehold Transcript*, July 18, 1941
6. *Monmouth Democrat*, May 18, 1939
7. *Monmouth Democrat*, May 3, 1939
8. *Freehold Transcript*, May 16, 1941
9. *Monmouth Democrat*, March 2, 1938
10. *Monmouth Democrat*, March 12, 1938
11. *Monmouth Democrat*, May 5, 1938

12. *Monmouth Democrat,* June 16, 1938
13. *Monmouth Democrat,* September 8, 1938
14. *Monmouth Democrat,* January 18, 1938
15. *Monmouth Democrat,* July 11, 1940
16. *Monmouth Democrat,* April 24, 1941
17. *Freehold Transcript,* October 17, 1941
18. *Monmouth Democrat,* June 16, 1938
19. *Asbury Park Press,* May 13, 1939
20. *Asbury Park Press,* May 1, 1958
21. Joel Hawkins and Terry Bertolino, *The House of David Baseball Team* (Charleston, South Carolina: Arcadia Publishing, 2000), 7.
22. Ryan Ferguson, "The religious sect that became baseball's answer to the Harlem Globetrotters," *The Guardian,* September 21, 2016.
23. *Freehold Transcript,* June 12, 1942
24. *Asbury Park Press,* May 1, 1939
25. *Asbury Park Press,* October 7, 1940
26. *Asbury Park Press,* May 20, 1941
27. *Asbury Park Press,* June 21, 1941
28. *Monmouth Democrat,* June 27, 1940
29. *Freehold Transcript,* June 23, 1944
30. *Freehold Transcript,* July 7, 1944
31. *Freehold Transcript,* September 1, 1944
32. *Freehold Transcript,* April 12, 1946
33. *Asbury Park Press,* August 12, 1946
34. *Freehold Transcript,* September 6, 1946
35. *Asbury Park Press,* August 1, 1947
36. *Asbury Park Press,* July 28, 1947
37. *Freehold Transcript,* August 29, 1947
38. *Asbury Park Press,* September 8, 1947
39. *Asbury Park Press,* August 1, 1957

40. *Asbury Park Press*, September 20, 1948

41. *Asbury Park Press*, October 2, 1948

42. *Asbury Park Press*, October 18, 1948

43. *Freehold Transcript*, October 22, 1948

44. *Freehold Transcript*, June 27, 1947

45. *Freehold Transcript*, August 3, 1946

46. *Freehold Transcript*, April 9, 1948

47. *Red Bank Register*, April 26, 1948

48. *Freehold Transcript*, May 14, 1948

49. *Asbury Park Press*, May 25, 1948

50. *Freehold Transcript*, August 17, 1950

51. *Freehold Transcript*, July 12, 1951

52. *Asbury Park Press*, May 26, 1950

53. *Freehold Transcript*, October 26, 1950

54. *Freehold Transcript*, August 24, 1950

55. *Freehold Transcript*, July 20, 1950

56. *Freehold Transcript*, June 28, 1951

57. *Freehold Transcript*, August 25, 1955

58. *Freehold Transcript*, May 20, 1954

59. *Freehold Transcript*, June 16, 1955

60. *Freehold Transcript*, April 17, 1958

61. *Freehold Transcript*, September 18, 1952

62. *Asbury Park Press*, July 30, 1973

Chapter 6: David "Dem" Cashion: One of Freehold's Best

1. *Freehold Transcript*, April 25, 1975

2. Ibid.

3. *Freehold Transcript*, February 28, 1936

4. James M. DiClerico and Barry J. Pavelec, *The Jersey Game* (New Brunswick, New Jersey: Rutgers University Press, 1991), 85–86.

5. George Will, *Men at Work* (Harper Perennial, 1990), 131.

6. *Monmouth Democrat*, June 29, 1933

7. *Monmouth Democrat*, June 24, 1933

8. *Monmouth Democrat*, October 10, 1935

9. *Monmouth Democrat*, May 13, 1937

10. Ibid.

11. *Monmouth Democrat*, October 14, 1937

12. Interview with Betty Cashion Henderson, January 31, 2001

13. *Freehold Transcript*, April 25, 1975

14. *Monmouth Democrat*, July 16, 1938

15. David Cashion's William J. Weiss Baseball Statistics Form, August 23, 1949

16. City Directory, R. L. Polk & Company, 1937

17. National Hall of Fame Archives, Cooperstown, New York

18. *Red Bank Daily Standard*, January 23, 1940

19. *Red Bank Daily Standard*, May 22, 1940

20. *Asbury Park Press*, July 20, 1940

21. *Central New Jersey Home News*, July 25, 1940

22. *Red Bank Daily Standard*, August 10, 1940

23. *Asbury Park Press*, August 17, 1940

24. *Matawan Journal*, October 3, 1940

25. *Monmouth Democrat*, October 3, 1940

26. *Asbury Park Press*, October 7, 1940

27. *Freehold Transcript*, October 10, 1941

28. *Asbury Park Press*, June 2, 1941

29. *Monmouth Democrat*, June 12, 1941

30. *Asbury Park Press*, October 13, 1941

31. *Freehold Transcript*, April 25, 1975

32. Dictionary of American Naval Fighting Ships

33. Kevin Coyne, *Marching Home* (Viking, 2003), 204.

Chapter 7: David "Dem" Cashion: He Lived it until the End

1. *Freehold Transcript*, April 25, 1975
2. *New York Times*, March 29, 2016
3. *Red Bank Daily Record*, September 16, 1946
4. *Asbury Park Press*, August 12, 1946
5. *Asbury Park Press*, September 2, 1947
6. *Asbury Park Press*, September 22, 1947
7. *Asbury Park Press*, September 29, 1947
8. *Asbury Park Press*, August 1957
9. *Asbury Park Press*, April 6, 1948
10. *Asbury Park Press*, April 11, 1948
11. *Monmouth Inquirer*, July 16, 1948
12. *Kingston Daily Freeman*, August 11, 1948
13. *Kingston Daily Freeman*, September 15, 1948
14. *Asbury Park Press*, September 20, 1948
15. *Freehold Transcript*, October 8, 1948
16. *Asbury Park Press*, October 18, 1948
17. *Monmouth Inquirer*, December 31, 1949
18. *Asbury Park Press*, September 12, 1949
19. "Brooklyn Bushwicks." Wikipedia, https://en. wikipedia.org/wiki/Brooklyn_Bushwicks
20. *Asbury Park Press*, May 22, 1950
21. *Asbury Park Press*, May 26, 1950
22. *Freehold Transcript*, October 26, 1950
23. Ibid.
24. *Asbury Park Press*, July 29, 1951
25. *Freehold Transcript*, June 1955; August 1957; May 1958
26. *Freehold Babe Ruth League 25th Anniversary Booklet*, July 1976
27. Interview with Betty Cashion Henderson, January 31, 2001
28. *Monmouth Inquirer*, May 10 and 17, 1951
29. *Monmouth Inquirer*, August 23, 1951

30. St. Rose of Lima Minstrel Program, March 1954
31. *Asbury Park Press*, July 5, 1953
32. *Monmouth Inquirer*, August 14, 1958
33. *Monmouth Inquirer*, May 16, 1963
34. *Asbury Park Press*, July 21, 1971
35. *Asbury Park Press*, July 30, 1973
36. *Monmouth Inquirer*, August 14, 1952
37. *Freehold Transcript*, August 14, 1959
38. *Asbury Park Press*, July 21, 1959
39. *Asbury Park Press*, June 14, 1965
40. *Freehold Transcript*, December 1, 1960
41. *Asbury Park Press*, January 4, 1973
42. *Freehold Transcript*, April 25, 1975
43. Ibid.
44. Ibid.
45. Ibid.
46. Ibid.
47. Ibid.
48. Interview with Ralph Steinberg, April 25, 2021
49. Interview with Barry Druesne, April 29, 2021
50. *Freehold Transcript*, April 25, 1975
51. *Asbury Park Press*, July 29, 1951

The "Tools of Ignorance"

1. *Freehold Transcript*, August 1926
2. Lee Allen, *100 Years of Baseball* (Bartholomew House, 1950), 171.
3. Ibid., p. 172.
4. Society for American Baseball Research, *Baseball Research Journal*,
5. Summer 2010, 2.

BIBLIOGRAPHY

Books

Allen, Lee. *100 Years of Baseball*. New York: Bartholomew House. 1950.

Casway, Jerrod I. *The Culture and Ethnicity of Nineteenth Century Baseball*. Jefferson, NC: McFarland & Company, 2017.

Chadwick, Henry. *Baseball Player: A Compendium of the Game*. New York: Irwin P. Beadle and Company. 1860.

Coyne, Kevin. *Marching Home*. New York: Viking Penguin. 2003.

Dawidoff, Nicholas. *The Catcher Was a Spy*. New York: Vintage Books. 1995.

DeClerico, James M. and Barry J. Pavelec. *The Jersey Game*. New Brunswick, NJ: Rutgers University Press. 1991.

Fitts, Robert K. *Banzai Babe Ruth*. Lincoln, NE: University of Nebraska Press. 2012.

Goldstein, Warren. *Playing for Keeps: A History of Early Baseball*. Ithaca, NY: Cornell University Press. 1989.

Halberstam, David. *October 1964*. New York: Villard Books. 1994.

Harris, Rick. *Brown University Baseball: a Legacy of the Game*. Charlestown, SC: The History Press. 2012.

Hawkins, Joel and Terry Bertolino. *The House of David Baseball Team*. Charlestown, SC: Arcadia Publishing. 2000.

James, Bill. *The New Bill James Historical Baseball Abstract*. New York: Free Press. 2008.

Jenkinson, Bill. *The Year Babe Ruth Hit 104 Home Runs*. New York: Carroll & Graf Publishers. 2007.

Kahn, Roger. *How the Weather Was*. New York: Harper & Row. 1973.

Kaufman, Louis, et al. *Moe Berg: Athlete, Scholar.* Boston: Little, Brown. 1974.

Kirsch, George B. *Baseball and Cricket.* Chicago: University of Illinois Press. 2007.

Kirsch, George B. *Baseball in Blue and Gray.* Princeton: Princeton University Press. 2003.

Lambert, Mike. *Eastern Shore League.* Charlestown, SC: Arcadia Publishing. 2010.

Leavy, Jane. *The Big Fella.* New York: Harper Collins. 2018.

Poekel, Charlie. *Babe & the Kid: The Legendary Story of Babe Ruth and Johnny Sylvester.* Charlestown, SC: The History Press. 2007.

Seymour, Harold and Dorothy Seymour Mills. *Baseball: The Early Years.* New York: Oxford University Press. 1960.

Seymour, Harold and Dorothy Seymour Mills. *Baseball: the People's Game.* New York: Oxford University Press. 1990.

Society of American Baseball Research *Summer Research Journal.* Phoenix. 2010.

Spaulding-Reach Official Baseball Guide 1941. New York: American Sports Publishing Company. 1941.

Spink, J. G. Taylor. *Official Baseball Guide and Record Book 1949.* St. Louis: 1949.

The Baseball Book. New York: Sports Illustrated Books. 2008.

Ward, John Montgomery. *Base-Ball, How to Become a Player.* Philadelphia: The Athletic Publishing Company. 1888.

Ward, Geoffrey C. and Ken Burns. *Baseball: An Illustrated History.* New York: Alfred A. Knopf. 1994.

Will, George. *Men at Work.* New York: HarperCollins. 1990.

Zinn, John G. *A Cradle of the National Pastime: New Jersey Baseball 1855–1880.* Princeton: Morven Museum & Garden. 2019.

Newspapers

Asbury Park Press. Asbury Park, NJ.

Central New Jersey Home News. New Brunswick, NJ.

Daily Record. Long Branch, NJ.

Freehold Transcript. Freehold, NJ.

Kingston Daily Freeman. Kingston, NY.

New York Times. New York, NY.

Matawan Journal. Matawan, NJ.

Monmouth Democrat. Freehold, NJ.

Monmouth Inquirer. Freehold. NJ.

Morning Call. Paterson, NJ.

Red Bank Daily Standard. Red Bank, NJ.

Red Bank Daily Record. Red Bank. NJ.

Other

Dictionary of American Naval Fighting Ships (website)

Negro League Baseball Players Accounts (website)

Eulogy for Betty Cashion Hendrickson, 2013

McNicholas Family Bible

Monmouth County Historical Association

National Baseball Hall of Fame Archives

Polk, R. L and Company. *City Directories.*

Freehold Babe Ruth League 25th Anniversary Booklet, Freehold, NJ, 1976.

100 Years: Our Hometown. Freehold, NJ, 2019.

Interviews

Barry Druesne

Betty Cashion Hendrickson

Frank Accisano

Harvey Whille

Norma Randolph

Ralph Steinberg

Roberta Schanck

Roger Kane

Wayne Cashion

Gene Glum

Fred "Booby" Quinn

INDEX

Note: Numbers followed by *f* refers to figures.

ABOUT THE AUTHOR

Glenn Cashion enjoyed a highly successful 40-year career serving in senior leadership positions—both stateside and globally—for several of the largest telecommunications companies in the U.S. These days, he is very active with Brown University's alumni association, the Marine Corps League, and several local historical organizations. Above all, he treasures time with his family.

Please consider leaving an online book review. Your honest feedback helps other readers discover the history of baseball in Freehold.

www.ingramcontent.com/pod-product-compliance
Lightning Source LLC
Chambersburg PA
CBHW020449130626
46549CB00001B/349